I0426710

The Power of Affirmations

Rewire Your Beliefs, Transform Your Mindset, Crack Code to Abundance & Manifest Success Through Affirmations

RAVINDER KAUR

Here is a gift for my readers.
If you want to be happy in your life then
collect this gift from my side.

Dedicated to

all those who are struggling in their
lives...trying to make it better

Acknowledgement

I am highly grateful to you as you are holding this book. I hope that the ideas and insights presented in this book will inspire you all to live a positive and fulfilling life. Thank you to everyone who has played a vital part in making this book on Inspiration a reality. Your support has been the driving force behind this endeavour, and I am truly grateful.

No achievement, big or small, is possible without the support of one's family, friends, and Almighty. It would not have been possible without the support of many people. My family has always been special to me; my mother and father have been a great source of inspiration. They have been encouraging me to chase my dreams. Their love and patience have been my constant source of positivity.

I also thank my husband Bharpur for his full support and assistance. I want to thank my husband for loving me the way I am, for being smart and for supporting me 100% which made this book possible. How can I forget the role my daughters played during writing this book?

I am indebted to everyone who directly or indirectly shaped my life, encouraged me, criticised me, and ultimately made me who I am, what I am and where I am today. I am thankful to all those whom I met along the way.

I am also immensely grateful to my friends and colleagues who have provided invaluable insights and feedback. Their diverse perspectives have enriched the content and made this book more comprehensive. Thank you for helping and bringing my vision to life. I would like to acknowledge the numerous authors, researchers, and experts whose work has inspired me.

Last but not the least, I would like to thank the Almighty. He supported me every time I was stuck with words. My belief in God helped me to go the extra mile towards a new life.

Table of Contents

Chapter 1

Introduction

"Affirmations are like seeds planted in soil. Poor soil, poor growth. Rich soil, abundant growth." - Louise Hay

How do you start your day?
I start mine with these affirmations.
Maybe they can help you too?

These are the small and positive affirmations which I daily recite after waking up in the morning to start my day on a high note...

I am Enough.
I love myself.
I am proud of myself.
I believe in me.
I deserve endless love and happiness.
I am stronger than my problems.
The past is over.

I hope these affirmations will help you the way they have helped me. Dear friends, in the hustle and bustle of daily life, we often find ourselves drowning in a sea of negativity, self-doubt, and stress. But what if I told you there is a

1

beacon of hope that can help you navigate these stormy waters? And that beacon of hope is the power of Affirmations.

Affirmations, those small but mighty statements, have the power to transform your life. Whether you're new to this world or a seasoned believer, let's explore the intriguing journey of affirmations and the remarkable impact they can have on your life. Affirmations are a great way to boost your self-confidence, vibrate yourself and increase your sense of well-being every day!

First things first, what are affirmations? They're short, positive statements that you repeat to yourself regularly. These statements can be about any aspect of your life: your goals, self-worth, relationships, health, or anything else you desire to improve. The magic lies in the fact that by repeatedly telling yourself these affirmations, you start to believe them, and they become your reality.

Affirmations are like the magical potions of our mind, little spells that can change the way we think, feel, and act. These short, positive statements, when repeated, start weaving their way into the fabric of our thoughts and beliefs. They can be about anything you desire — your dreams, your worth, your relationships, or your well-being. The beauty lies in their simplicity; affirmations can turn your aspirations into reality.

Let's talk about one of the most common uses of affirmations: boosting self-confidence. We all have moments of self-doubt, but affirmations can help build a strong foundation of self-belief. For instance, repeating, "I am confident and capable," can gradually shift your mindset and help you tackle challenges with more assurance.

Affirmations are not just about changing your self-perception; they can also help you achieve your goals. When you focus your thoughts on what you want to accomplish and truly believe it's possible, you set the stage for success. For example, if your goal is to run a marathon, an affirmation like, "I am a strong and resilient runner," can keep you motivated and on track.

Affirmations can enhance your relationships in addition to helping you become a better version of yourself. You can encourage positivity in your interactions with others by reciting affirmations. Watch how improving your relationships with friends, family, and coworkers by simply declaring, "I am a great listener and communicator," will improve your relationships.

How can you then incorporate affirmations into your everyday activities? You'd be surprised at how easy it is. Pick a few affirmations that speak to you personally to start. They ought to be upbeat, in the moment, and specific to you. Next, every day, take a quiet moment to say these affirmations to yourself. They might be spoken aloud or quietly in your head. Some people enjoy writing their affirmations down or even using them to make vision boards. Affirmations provide a ray of brightness and hope in a world full of negativity, worry, and self-doubt. They serve as your cheerleaders, always reassuring you of your value, your potential, and your aspirations. Why not try them and see how they can change your life, one thought at a time?

In a world filled with constant change and challenges, the human mind holds a remarkable power—the power to shape our reality through the spoken word. This power, known as affirmations, has been harnessed by cultures throughout history and continues to inspire individuals on their journey of self-discovery and personal transformation.

Affirmations are not mere words but profound declarations that have the potential to reshape our thoughts, emotions, and actions. In the modern era, the concept of affirmations has not only endured but flourished. It has been embraced by visionaries, thinkers, and countless individuals seeking to unlock their full potential. It has found a place in the realm of psychology, where researchers have delved into the science behind the transformative effects of these simple yet profound statements.

This book, "The Power of Affirmations," is your guide to understanding, crafting, and harnessing the potential of affirmations to create positive change in your life. Whether you are looking to boost self-esteem, achieve your goals, or find inner peace, the journey begins here.

In the pages that follow, we will explore the psychology behind affirmations, provide practical techniques for creating personalized affirmations, and share inspiring stories of individuals who have witnessed the remarkable impact of these powerful declarations. Whether you are new to the world of affirmations or a seasoned practitioner, this book offers a comprehensive roadmap to harness the incredible power of your own words to transform your reality. Before implementing the Affirmations, kindly go through my life transformation journey.

Chapter 2

My Life Transformation

"The more you praise and celebrate your life, the more there is in life to celebrate."

- Oprah Winfrey

Life is a beautiful journey full of ups and downs; without these, doctors will declare you a dead body. A straight line is fatal in medical terms. There is a need to work on the curved line i.e., smile. It is a wonderful expression in this beautiful world that can create miracles in life. A single smile to a stranger can divert their mind from their pains and they will start thinking about you. Who are you? Why did you pass a smile to them? So, start spreading your beautiful smile to the beautiful souls of this beautiful planet.

A smile can change the mood and energy of those around you. If we talk about life, it is not the same all the time. You cannot be happy all the time. There may be some occasions when you will feel sad, depressed or upset over petty issues. The only thing is to change your perspective of looking at things.

I strongly believe in the words of Wayne Dyer, "Change the way you look at things and the things you look at change." When you change the way, you see the world; when your intentions are positive and powerful; when you only search for the good, then your life transforms into the amazing adventure it was designed to be. My belief in me made me who I am today.

Nothing is permanent in this world; everything is evolving so am I. I belong to a middle-class family in Punjab. I have experienced almost everything in my life. Our life completely takes a new shape when we decide to take a new step in our life: getting married. The same happened with me, moving to a new family, with new people, at a new place, different language as well as different thinking.

I know that the five fingers of a hand are not equal still, they make a fist. Then how can people from different regions be the same? I know that India is known for its unity in diversity. Varied cultures, different languages, unique thinking, and different people; this diversity makes our India more Incredible. I am proud to be an Indian.

Life is a journey of connecting with different people during various phases of life. I have connected with so many people. Some resonated with me well and some did not. Some gave me the direction to start my life from scratch and to live my dreams. However, due to some responsibilities after marriage, I kept my dreams aside and started focusing on my family.

One day, in 2018, I was busy writing my thoughts in my diary. Then, I realised that now I can start working on my dreams and that day was the first day of my transformation journey. My transformation journey started while I was reading the book "Aspire Before You Expire" by Ujjwal Patni. That book is a completely mind-blowing book. I completed that book in four days and those four days were sufficient to push me towards my dreams. While reading that book, I was stuck in one place when the author provided one activity to was to write my obituary.

It was difficult for me to write that. With some courage, I picked one paper and pen and started writing my obituary. Initially, I was thinking about what I could start after 12 years of my marriage, being a homemaker, with no job experience. So, I was feeling a bit demotivated, and then I thought why not start writing something? I started with free writing. With some consistent days of writing, I got the courage to write a book. As you know there is a famous Chinese proverb, "A thousand-mile journey always starts with a small step." That first step gave birth to an Author when I launched my first book "Live Life as Your Last Inning" in November 2019.

After launching my first book, I was not sure how to promote that book due to my limited circle. As you all know 2020 was the pandemic year of history. It gave me sufficient time to research and learn new skills that aided in my networking. I learnt self-publishing skills. Learning one skill at a time created curiosity to learn more skills. In 2020, I launched my second book "Positive Alphabets of Life." After launching my first two books I became unstoppable. Then I wrote my Third Fiction book "Quit Like a Strong Woman."

Even after publishing three books, I wanted to know more as I was not connected with my readers. Then I started learning Marketing as I was not aware of the advertising process. After joining Author Freedom Hub, I got a like-minded community and received motivation and constant push to publish books in series. With unconditional love and support, now I am a Self-Published author of 9 books with the 9th book being in your hands.

Thank you so much for showing your love, blessings and support to me. As it matters a lot to me. That was just a trailer of my transformation journey. The movie is not over yet. I will cover the behind-the-scenes in my upcoming books. I am sure you have the curiosity to transform your life with affirmations. You can use the same affirmations in your life that I am reciting daily or you can create your own as per your requirements.

Excitement to learn more makes me a life-long learner and it works for all. Never stop learning, and live your life as your last inning. If you know that you do not have your tomorrow, then you will live to the fullest and embrace the beauty of life every day. My consistency and chasing my dreams worked wonders with affirmations as I became an unstoppable and lifelong learner. I strongly believe nothing is impossible if we follow the process and adopt good habits that will create an abundance of Success and Wealth in life. There is always a need to think out of the box. When you step out of your comfort zone and accomplish something that you wish to achieve will lead you to achieve more and more. This is your continuous motivation and your real mentor in life. I believe,

Consistency + Habits= Success

Chapter 3

Affirmations...WHAT??

"The most powerful words in the universe are the words you say to yourself." -
Marie Forleo

In the 17th century, a French thinker named René Descartes said, "I think, therefore I am." Later, in the early 1900s, another French person, psychologist Émile Coué, came up with something called the Coué method. That method suggested people to repeat the following, "Every day, in every way, I'm getting better and better" 20 times at the start and end of each day. It worked wonders.

Affirmations are like the high-fives you give yourself daily. They are short, positive statements or phrases that are intended to boost your mood and confidence. These affirmations work by nudging your mind towards more positive thoughts, whether you whisper to yourself, "I am capable and strong," or repeat, "I am enough," in the mirror. Positive affirmations are a form of self-help. Practising daily positive affirmations can help you overcome fear and self-doubt and reduce self-sabotage. Daily positive Affirmations help you believe in yourself and what you can achieve.

I suggested one of my friends practice affirmations. She has always been insecure about her body. So, I sent all the affirmations that I practice and some other affirmations that could be helpful to her.

Recently, she told me those affirmations did not work.

Why does it not work?

Because you don't add feelings into it.

Whatever you are saying, you should believe in that, only then affirmation works. Suppose I say I AM BEAUTIFUL, then I will look at my beautiful smile, my sparkling eyes. I will feel beautiful from the INSIDE. Rather than looking at my pimples and feel upset. Make sure your words match with emotions. They should not contradict each other.

What we feel about ourselves inside we reflect outside the world and to the other person. For instance, one day I was getting ready to go to the salon. As I was getting ready, I said some of the affirmations like:

I AM CONFIDENT.
I AM BEAUTIFUL.
I LOVE MY BODY.
I LOVE MYSELF.

I said all this while looking into the mirror, making a good body posture.

When I reached the salon, a man came to me and complimented "You were looking like a doll coming down the stairs, So Pretty."

It was a genuine compliment; I could see his eyes were sparkling.

Now here is what happened I was self-aware about my body; I was reflecting my confidence towards him.

So, I smiled and thanked him.

Adding EMOTIONS to your affirmations is a must.

Emotions mean Energy in motion so when you add that in your affirmations, it works effectively.

Henry Ford once said: *"Whether you think you can, or you think you can't - you're right."* It means that the view you have of yourself will profoundly affect the way you lead your life. For example, if you believe you can think more positively, you can make it happen. Conversely, if you don't believe in the power of positive thinking, then it doesn't matter how much others will tell you how great the benefits are. How can you think more positively? Start nurturing a "growth mindset" (versus a fixed mindset). If there's something about your mindset you don't like, the good news is - you can change it for the better.

Here I want to remind the thoughts of Wayne Dyer, "Change the way you look at things and the things you look at change." When you change the way you see the world; when your intentions are positive and powerful; when you only search for the good, then your life transforms into the amazing adventure it was designed to be.

The only way is to use Affirmations. They serve as your cheering section, pushing out negative thoughts and replacing them with positive ones. The more you say them, the more they sink in, like seeds of positivity planted in your mind. They are your secret weapon for feeling more confident, upbeat, and prepared to face whatever life throws at you.

Positive affirmations are short, powerful statements that can help you overcome negative thoughts and beliefs. They are a powerful tool for self-improvement and can help you achieve your goals and live a happier, more fulfilling life. Affirmations are positive statements that you repeat to yourself to change your mindset and beliefs. They are often used in meditation or as part of a daily routine to help you focus on the present moment and cultivate a positive attitude. Affirmations can be used to overcome negative self-talk, boost self-esteem, and improve overall well-being.

How do Affirmations Work?

Consider affirmations to be seeds that you plant in your mental garden. These seeds, when nurtured with repetition, grow into beliefs, influencing your mindset. Saying things like "I am capable," "I am resilient," or "I choose to be happy" is like talking to your subconscious. They shift your attention from self-doubt to self-assurance, gradually shaping your perspective on life.

Do you look in the mirror before leaving the house in the morning? According to Louise Hay, an affirmations and positive thinking expert, the morning is a great opportunity to practice mirror work, in which you recite affirmations while looking at yourself in the mirror.

Hay believes morning is the best time to determine how you want the rest of the day to go. It is why positive morning affirmations can be very powerful—and a great opportunity to practice repeating them in the mirror. Here are some of her suggestions:

1. I am beautiful and everybody loves me.

2. Life brings me only good experiences. I am open to new and wonderful changes.

3. I feel glorious, dynamic energy. I am active and alive.

4. Every experience I have is perfect for my growth.

5. Today I create a wonderful day and a wonderful new future.

6. Abundance flows freely through me.

7. My self-esteem is high because I honour who I am.

Benefits of Positive Affirmations

Some of the most notable benefits include:

- Increased self-confidence and self-esteem
- Improved focus and motivation
- Reduced stress and anxiety
- Improved overall well-being
- Increased resilience and ability to overcome challenges

How to Use Affirmations?

There are many ways to incorporate affirmations into your daily routine. Here are a few suggestions:

- **Write them down:** Write your affirmations on sticky notes and place them around your home or workspace where you will see them often.

- **Repeat them in the mirror:** Stand in front of a mirror and repeat your affirmations to yourself. This can help you connect with the words and believe them more deeply.

- **Use them in meditation:** Incorporate affirmations into your meditation practice by repeating them silently or out loud during your practice.

- **Create a daily affirmation ritual:** Set aside a few minutes each day to sit quietly and repeat your affirmations to yourself.

Never underestimate the power of positive affirmations.

When you say I can do, you will do it.

When you say, I cannot do it, you will not do it.

It is because your mind obeys the thoughts you feed into it.

Your mind is like a pet dog. Your pet dog obeys whatever you command it to do. Likewise, your mind also obeys whatever you tell it to do.

This is the reason you should always be positive in your life. You might be facing the toughest phase in your life. But you must not let go of your trying.

You should command your mind "Do it."

You should command your mind "Never stop trying."

You should command your mind "I am capable."

Your positive affirmations will do the rest for your success.

Examples of Positive Affirmations

Here are some examples of positive affirmations that you can use in your daily life:

- I am capable and strong.
- I am worthy of love and happiness.
- I am confident and successful.
- I am surrounded by love and support.
- I am grateful for all that I have.
- I am in control of my thoughts and emotions.
- I can achieve my goals.
- I am deserving of all the good things in my life.
- I am resilient and can overcome any challenge.
- I am proud of who I am and all that I have accomplished.

Chapter 4

Importance of Affirmations

"Affirmations are to the mind what exercise is to the body."
- Brian Tracy

Affirmations are like giving yourself a daily pep talk for a better life. It is about repeating positive statements to yourself that can change the way you think and feel. When you say things like "I am capable" or "I am confident," it is like planting seeds of self-belief in your mind. Over time, these thoughts grow and help you tackle challenges, boost your self-esteem, and stay motivated.

It is a simple but powerful way to remind yourself that you have the potential to achieve your goals and overcome obstacles. So, if you want to feel more positive, try using affirmations to give yourself that extra dose of encouragement every day. Affirmations help in developing:

- **Positive Mindset:** Daily affirmations help instill and reinforce a positive mindset. By consistently focusing on positive statements, individuals can shift their thought patterns away from negativity, self-doubt, and pessimism.

- **Self-Esteem and Self-Confidence:** Affirmations designed to boost self-esteem and self-confidence can have a profound impact on one's self-image. They encourage self-worth and a belief in one's abilities.

- **Mental Resilience:** Daily affirmations contribute to mental resilience by promoting a more optimistic and empowered outlook. This can help individuals better cope with challenges and setbacks.

- **Stress Reduction:** Affirmations can serve as a tool for managing stress and anxiety. By focusing on calming and positive statements, individuals can reduce the impact of stressors on their mental and emotional well-being.

- **Goal Achievement:** Affirmations are effective for goal setting and goal achievement. When people repeatedly affirm their ability to reach specific objectives, they tend to stay motivated and committed to those goals.

- **Emotional Balance:** Daily affirmations can enhance emotional balance by encouraging positive emotions and reducing negative ones.

This can lead to greater emotional well-being and mental health.

- **Increased Focus:** By using affirmations that emphasize concentration and productivity, individuals can improve their focus and work more efficiently, ultimately leading to increased success in their endeavours.

- **Improved Self-Image:** Over time, daily affirmations can lead to an improved self-image and a greater sense of self-acceptance. This can help individuals let go of self-criticism and embrace self-love.

- **Enhanced Relationships:** Affirmations that focus on empathy, patience, and effective communication can improve relationships with others. By fostering positive qualities, individuals can create more harmonious connections.

- **Physical Health:** Research has shown that affirmations can have a positive impact on physical health. By reducing stress and promoting well-being, they contribute to overall health.

- **Confidence in Decision-Making:** Affirmations that focus on self-trust and confidence in decision-making can help individuals make choices more assertively and with greater conviction.

- **Mindfulness and Presence:** Daily affirmations combined with mindfulness practices encourage living in the present moment, fostering greater awareness and appreciation for life as it unfolds.

- **Motivation:** Repeated affirmations of motivation and determination can boost the drive to act and work toward one's goals and dreams.

- **Gratitude and Positivity:** Affirmations related to gratitude encourage individuals to appreciate and focus on the positive aspects of their lives, which leads to a more joyful and content existence.

- **Personal Growth:** Daily affirmations can be a powerful tool for personal growth and development. They encourage individuals to embrace change, explore their potential, and continuously strive to become the best version of themselves.

- **Habit Formation:** When used consistently, daily affirmations can become a habit themselves. This habit reinforces positive thinking and personal empowerment.

- **Positive Self-Talk:** Daily affirmations essentially serve as a form of positive self-talk. This self-talk becomes a powerful inner dialogue that encourages self-empowerment and resilience. When faced with challenges or self-doubt, the positive inner voice can provide reassurance and encouragement.

- **Emotional Regulation:** Daily affirmations can be a valuable tool for emotional regulation. They help individuals become more aware of their emotions and offer a constructive way to manage them. When individuals repeat affirmations that promote emotional well-being, they are better equipped to navigate the ups and downs of life with greater equanimity.

- **Increased Productivity:** Affirmations can improve productivity by boosting motivation and focus. When individuals remind themselves daily of their goals, capabilities, and aspirations, they are more likely to act and stay on track. The increased self-belief that affirmations provide can be a driving force behind improved productivity.

- **Positive Habits:** Affirmations can also be used to reinforce the adoption of positive habits. For example, if someone wants to develop a habit of regular exercise, they can use affirmations like "I am committed to my daily workout routine." By repeating such affirmations, they internalize and reinforce their commitment to the desired habit.

- **Strengthened Relationships:** Affirmations that emphasize qualities like empathy, kindness, and communication can have a transformative effect on relationships. By affirming these qualities daily, individuals can become more emotionally available and compassionate in their interactions with others.

- **Resilience in Adversity:** Daily affirmations contribute to resilience in the face of adversity. When challenges arise, individuals who have ingrained affirmations about their strength and adaptability are better equipped to weather the storm with a sense of hope and determination.

- **Overcoming Limiting Beliefs:** Affirmations are particularly effective for dismantling limiting beliefs. These self-imposed limitations can often hold individuals back from realizing their full potential. Affirmations that challenge and replace these limiting beliefs can lead to significant personal growth.

- **Intention and Focus:** Daily affirmations set the intention and focus for the day. When individuals begin their day with positive and empowering statements, they are more likely to align their actions with those intentions and stay focused on what truly matters to them.

- **Personal Empowerment:** The consistent practice of daily affirmations fosters personal empowerment. It reinforces the notion that individuals have the power to shape their own lives and destiny. This sense of agency can be a driving force behind pursuing one's dreams and ambitions.

- **Improved Mental Health:** Affirmations can be a valuable complement to mental health practices. They can be integrated into mindfulness and meditation routines, helping individuals manage conditions such as anxiety, depression, and stress.

- **Optimism and Happiness:** Affirmations encourage a more optimistic outlook on life. By training the mind to focus on the good, individuals can increase their overall happiness and life satisfaction.

- **A Lifelong Tool:** One of the most significant advantages of daily affirmations is that they are a tool for life. As individuals grow and evolve, they can adapt their affirmations to reflect their changing goals, challenges, and aspirations. This lifelong practice contributes to ongoing personal development and well-being.

- **Self-Compassion:** Affirmations can foster self-compassion. By repeating affirmations that encourage self-love and kindness, individuals learn to treat themselves with the same care and understanding they might extend to others. This self-compassion is a powerful source of emotional resilience.

- **Cultivating Gratitude:** Daily affirmations that express gratitude help individuals appreciate the abundance in their lives. This practice shifts the focus from what is lacking to what is present, promoting contentment and fulfilment.

- **Adaptability and Change:** Daily affirmations promote adaptability and a positive attitude toward change. They can remind individuals that change is a natural part of life and that they have the strength and resilience to adapt to new circumstances.

- **Promoting Affirmative Action:** Affirmations not only shape the mind but also influence behaviour. When individuals repeatedly affirm their capabilities, they are more likely to take affirmative action aligned with those beliefs, leading to tangible progress and growth.

- **Strengthening Identity:** Affirmations can play a role in strengthening one's identity. By reinforcing positive qualities and values, individuals gain a deeper sense of who they are and who they want to become.

- **Supporting Personal and Professional Growth:** Whether applied to personal or professional goals, daily affirmations are a versatile tool for growth. They can boost confidence, motivation, and a sense of direction in various life areas, from career advancement to personal development.

- **Reduction of Negative Self-Talk:** Negative self-talk is a common source of self-sabotage. Affirmations provide a counterbalance to this negativity by offering positive and constructive alternatives. Over time, individuals may find that their inner critic becomes less prominent.

- **Enhanced Creativity:** Positive affirmations can boost creativity by promoting a mindset that is open to new ideas, free from self-doubt, and unafraid of experimentation.

- **Improved Communication:** Affirmations that focus on effective communication can improve interpersonal relationships. When individuals affirm their communication skills daily, they become more confident in expressing their thoughts and feelings.

- **Building a Supportive Internal Environment:** Daily affirmations create an internal environment of support and encouragement. This inner cheerleader motivates individuals to keep going, even when external circumstances are challenging.

- **Enhancing Decision-Making:** By affirming one's capacity for sound judgment and decision-making, individuals can navigate choices with greater self-assuredness and clarity.

- **Heightened Self-Awareness:** Affirmations can promote self-awareness by encouraging individuals to reflect on their values, strengths, and areas for improvement. This introspective practice deepens personal growth.

- **Fostering a Sense of Purpose:** Affirmations that focus on purpose can help individuals connect with their passions and align their actions with a sense of meaning and direction.

The beauty of daily affirmations lies in their adaptability to individual needs and goals. Whether you are looking to boost your self-esteem, manage stress, achieve personal or professional goals, or simply maintain a positive outlook on life, daily affirmations can serve as an invaluable tool for fostering self-empowerment and overall well-being. They are a simple yet profound practice that can yield lasting positive changes in your life.

Positive affirmations are phrases you say to yourself that you believe to be true. You can use a positive affirmation to replace a negative thought, to change behaviour, or to challenge limiting beliefs. It is a way of reprogramming your subconscious mind. For example, let's say you want to lose weight, and you could use a positive affirmation as one of several tools to make yourself healthier. You would repeatedly say, "I am healthy," or "I eat healthy foods," or "I exercise regularly."

Whenever you think of a negative thought, like "I'll never lose the weight," you can say a positive affirmation instead. That will reinforce your new mindset of health.

You can also make sure your environment reinforces your affirmation. For example, you can put a new fruit and vegetable tray on your kitchen counter. Every time you have a snack, you can look at the tray and remember, "I'm eating healthy."

In the same way, you can make your home a "healthier" place. Replace your coffee table with a simple glass of water. Every time you sit on the couch, drink a glass of water, and say a positive affirmation.

- I am beautiful inside out.
- I excel in everything that I do.
- I can reach any goal I set for myself.
- All that I need is within me.
- I am worthy of my desires and dreams.

After reading various benefits of affirmations, you would love to apply them in your life. Wait, wait, before taking action you need to learn the various types of affirmations that you will read in the coming pages.

Chapter 5

Types of Affirmations

"Your life does not get better by chance; it gets better by change." - Jim Rohn

Let us learn something new on this transformative journey as we delve deep into the practical applications of affirmations. Together, we will unlock the door to a brighter, more empowered future—one affirmation at a time. Affirmations come in various types, and they can be tailored to suit different goals and purposes. Here are some common types of affirmations:

1. Positive Affirmations: These are statements framed positively to cultivate a more optimistic outlook and mindset. Positive affirmations are powerful statements that you can say to yourself to help achieve your goals and improve your life. Repeating positive affirmations can help to increase your confidence, motivation, and focus. Some examples of positive affirmations include:

- I am confident and capable.
- I am worthy of love and happiness.

- I am grateful for all the goodness in my life.
- I am strong and capable of overcoming any obstacle.

2.   Negative Affirmations (Reversals): These affirmations aim to counteract and replace negative self-talk or beliefs. They involve transforming negative thoughts into positive ones. For example, changing "I'm not good enough" to "I am more than enough."

3.   Present Tense Affirmations: These affirmations are stated as if the desired outcome is already happening in the present. They reinforce the belief that the desired state is currently true. For example, "I am living a fulfilling life."

4.   Future Tense Affirmations: Future tense affirmations focus on what one intends to achieve or experience in the future. They instill a sense of hope and anticipation. For example, "I will achieve my goals and dreams."

5.   Affirmations for Specific Goals: These affirmations are tailored to a particular objective, whether it is related to career, health, relationships, or personal development. For example, "I am steadily progressing in my career."

6.   Affirmations for Health and Wellness: These affirmations focus on physical and mental health, promoting well-being and healing. For example, "I am radiantly healthy in mind and body."

7. Affirmations for Self-Esteem and Confidence: These affirmations target self-worth and self-assurance. They help build self-esteem and boost confidence. For example, "I am worthy of love and respect."

8. Affirmations for Abundance and Prosperity: These affirmations focus on attracting wealth, abundance, and financial success. For example, "I am a magnet for prosperity."

9. Affirmations for Love and Relationships: These affirmations aim to improve or attract positive, healthy relationships. For example, "I attract loving and supportive people into my life."

10. Affirmations for Stress Reduction: These affirmations assist in managing stress and promoting relaxation. For example, "I am calm and balanced in stressful situations."

11. Affirmations for Creativity: These affirmations inspire creativity and innovation. They can help overcome creative blocks. For example, "I am a creative genius, and my ideas flow effortlessly."

12. Affirmations for Gratitude: These affirmations encourage the practice of gratitude, promoting a positive outlook and appreciation for life's blessings. For example, "I am grateful for the abundance in my life."

13. Affirmations for Personal Growth: These affirmations focus on self-improvement and personal development. They instill a commitment to continuous growth. For example, "I am constantly evolving and becoming the best version of myself."

14. Affirmations for Mindfulness: These affirmations support mindfulness and presence in the moment. They can enhance meditation practices. For example, "I am fully present and at peace in this moment."

15. Affirmations for Overcoming Fears: These affirmations target specific fears or phobias, helping individuals confront and conquer them. For example, "I am fearless and capable of facing my fears."

16. Affirmations for Spiritual Growth: These affirmations focus on spiritual development, fostering a deeper connection with one's inner self or a higher power. For example, "I am aligned with my spiritual purpose."

17.   Daily Affirmations: These are short, concise affirmations designed to be part of a daily routine. They set a positive tone for the day and help maintain a positive mindset. For example, "Today is a new day filled with opportunities."

18.   Affirmations   for   Healing: These affirmations focus on physical or emotional healing. They can be used to speed up recovery or to promote emotional well-being. For example, "I am healing and getting stronger every day."

19.   Affirmations   for   Forgiveness: Forgiveness affirmations help individuals let go of grudges and resentment, promoting emotional freedom and inner peace. For example, "I release all resentment and forgive those who have hurt me."

20.   Affirmations for Stress Management: These affirmations are specifically aimed at reducing stress levels and promoting relaxation. For example, "I am in control of my stress, and I choose to stay calm and balanced."

21.   Affirmations for Weight Loss: These affirmations support individuals in their weight loss journeys by fostering a positive body image and motivation for healthy habits. For example, "I love and care for my body, making healthy choices every day."

22. Affirmations for Overcoming Addictions: These affirmations are geared toward helping individuals overcome various forms of addiction, such as smoking, overeating, or substance abuse. For example, "I am free from the grip of addiction, and I choose a healthy life."

23. Affirmations for Confidence in Public Speaking: Public speaking affirmations help boost confidence and reduce anxiety when speaking in front of an audience. For example, "I am a confident and engaging speaker, captivating my audience."

24. Affirmations for Academic Success: These affirmations assist students in boosting their motivation, focus, and self-belief to achieve academic excellence. For example, "I am a diligent learner, and I excel in my studies."

25. Affirmations for Parenting: Parenting affirmations help parents stay patient, loving, and supportive while raising their children. For example, "I am a loving and capable parent, guiding my children with compassion."

26. Affirmations for Letting Go of the Past: These affirmations aid in releasing past regrets and traumas, allowing individuals to move forward with a sense of freedom. For example, "I release the past and embrace a bright future."

27. Affirmations for Decision-Making: Decision-making affirmations impart confidence in one's ability to make sound choices and trust their judgment. For example, "I trust my intuition and make decisions with clarity."

28. Affirmations for Confidence in Relationships: These affirmations promote self-assuredness and healthy communication within relationships. For example, "I am confident in my ability to connect and communicate in meaningful relationships."

29. Affirmations for Resilience: Resilience affirmations strengthen one's ability to bounce back from setbacks and challenges. For example, "I am resilient, and I grow stronger with every obstacle I face."

30. Affirmations for Creativity in Problem-Solving: These affirmations boost creative thinking and problem-solving skills. For example, "I am a creative thinker, finding innovative solutions to challenges."

31. Affirmations for Letting Go of Perfectionism: Perfectionism affirmations help individuals embrace imperfections and release the need for everything to be flawless. For example, "I embrace my imperfections and appreciate my uniqueness."

32. Affirmations for Empowerment: Empowerment affirmations focus on feeling empowered to take control of one's life and destiny. For example, "I am empowered to create the life I desire."

Choosing affirmations that resonate with your goals and values is important.

Customizing affirmations to suit your unique needs and aspirations can maximize their effectiveness in creating positive change in your life.

Remember that the effectiveness of affirmations lies not only in the words themselves but in the sincerity and consistency with which they are practised.

Choose affirmations that resonate with your specific goals and aspirations, and incorporate them into your daily routine to experience their positive impact on your life.

Chapter 6

3 Ps of Affirmations

"Your mind is just like a garden; your thoughts are the seeds. You can grow flowers or you can grow weeds. Decide what you want." -Ravinder Kaur

When we say "I am this and that over and over again," we are creating a new reality for ourselves – one that allows us to experience the life that we want to live. You can use affirmations to change your negative thinking patterns and replace or reframe them with positive ones!

During the last four to five years, in my yoga session, I affirm, "I am happy, I am healthy and I am improving every day in every way." All credit goes to my Health and Yoga-certified Coach Saurabh Bothra. This way I am training my mind that I am happy and whole day I perform all my daily chores productively and before the end of the day I feel I am an achiever and have achieved my daily tasks efficiently.

Undoubtedly, positive affirmations are an easy way to make your life better! They can help improve your self-esteem, bring clarity into situations in which you find yourself stuck or confused, increase productivity at work and home (and other areas), create more energy and motivation in all aspects of your life...the list goes on!

Affirmations are like the architects of our thoughts, constructing the blueprint of our mindset and influencing the course of our lives. To truly grasp their transformative potential, let's explore the three fundamental principles often referred to as the "3 Ps of Affirmations." But before affirming yourself, you need to prepare – what are those 3 Ps of affirmation? These are:

- Present tense: Be More Present,
- Personal: Be More Personal and
- Positive: Build Positive Affirmations.

First P is Present

Use present tense in your affirmation while you are writing: What you want to affirm right now and the outcome of your affirmation. Do not use future tense it will simply remind you that this is what you want in general, 5 or 10 years from now – no good! Name three things that support or strengthen your affirmation: People, things, or events, objective realities like the sun rising every morning, etc. Be as specific as possible –see yourself achieve each aspect.

When we affirm in the present, we are essentially telling our minds that the change we seek is not a distant dream but a current reality. Consider the difference between saying "I will be confident" and "I am confident." The latter brings the assurance of confidence into the present, influencing our thoughts and actions in the 'now'.

The present tense inspires a sense of urgency and conviction in our affirmations. It is a call to live in the moment we wish to create, fostering a proactive mindset. Affirming in the present aligns our intentions with our current reality, acting as a catalyst for positive change.

Second P is Personal

Affirmations, to be truly transformative, must be deeply personal. The second 'P' emphasizes tailoring affirmations to reflect your unique goals, values, and aspirations. Personalized affirmations resonate more profoundly because they address your specific journey and speak directly to your experiences.

Crafting personal affirmations involves introspection and self-awareness. Consider the areas of your life where you seek growth, improvement, or transformation. Whether it is enhancing self-esteem, navigating challenges, or cultivating relationships, the power of personal affirmations lies in their ability to directly address your specific needs.

For example, instead of a generic affirmation like "I am successful," personalize it to align with your goals: "I am achieving success in my career and feeling fulfilled in my accomplishments." This tailored approach connects your affirmations to your unique narrative, making them more potent and relevant.

Personal affirmations also act as a reminder of your inherent worth and potential. By acknowledging and affirming your different strengths and capabilities, you reinforce a positive self-image. This, in turn, propels you towards actions that align with your affirmed values and aspirations.

When you write your daily affirmation, you need to be more personal. Write an affirmation about yourself! Imagine how good it feels to be more a confident version of yourself – write that emotional state with positivity.

You can combine both positive and negative affirmations with these two types of sentences: I like the way _____ (whatever) turns out (how you want things to develop) or rather not/let's stop doing this nonsense now. Your wording is up to you.

Third P is Positive

The third 'P' underscores the undeniable influence of positivity in affirmations. Positivity is the life force that propels our thoughts towards growth and abundance. Positive affirmations operate on the principle that what we focus on expands, and by deliberately directing our thoughts towards the positive, we shape a more optimistic mindset.

Positive affirmations are not about denying challenges or setbacks; rather, they are about choosing empowering perspectives in the face of adversity. Consider a situation where you are confronted with a professional challenge.

You need to use a positive word or phrase in your affirmation. It will remind you that this is what you want and it will also inspire you to keep going! Try these examples: I am confident, I am successful, I am powerful, I am beautiful, I am healthy, etc. Positive words and phrases are always better than negative ones.

Instead of affirming, "I won't fail," shift towards the positive with "I am capable of overcoming challenges and learning from them." This technique is very simple and easy to use. Just visualize yourself being successful in the future and being happy with what you have achieved.

Positivity in affirmations also cultivates a mindset of gratitude. Integrating statements that express gratitude for the present and anticipation for the future enhances the overall impact of affirmations. For instance, "I am grateful for the opportunities in my life, and I eagerly welcome the abundance that is flowing towards me."

Moreover, the language of positivity in affirmations is contagious. When you consistently affirm positive statements, you radiate that positivity to those around you. It becomes a ripple effect, influencing not only your mindset but also the energy you bring into your relationships and interactions.

In conclusion, the 3 Ps of Affirmations—Present, Personal, and Positive—form a dynamic framework for harnessing the transformative power of this simple yet profound tool. By grounding affirmations in the present, personalizing them to your unique journey, and infusing them with positivity, you pave the way for a mindset shift that can accelerate personal growth and create the reality you desire. Affirmations, when crafted with intention and lived with conviction, have the potential to reshape not only your thoughts but also the trajectory of your life. Embrace the 3 Ps and let the journey of positive transformation begin.

Chapter 7

Physical Body

"Affirmations are the daily Vitamins and Minerals for the mind, nourishing it with positivity and strength." -Ravinder Kaur

Positive affirmations can be a super refreshing way to use positive self-talk capable of reversing negative internal messages and motivating ourselves. Whether you are seeking a means of coping with anxiety, want to get yourself pumped for something, or just want to be more optimistic in general, try coming up with your affirmations. In this chapter, I will share some specific affirmations for weight loss, anti-ageing, weight gain and healthy hair.

Weight Loss

Many people are worried about the excess body weight. They are following different strategies like going to the gym, and following a strict diet but still cannot see any change in their body weight. Here are some generic affirmations for weight loss:

- I am releasing excess weight and embracing a healthy, vibrant body.

- Every day, I am moving closer to my ideal weight and feeling amazing.
- My body is a temple, I nourish it with healthy choices.
- I can achieve my weight loss goals and maintain a healthy lifestyle.
- I choose foods that fuel my body and support my weight loss journey.
- I am committed to regular exercise, which strengthens my body and aids in weight loss.
- I celebrate every milestone on my weight loss journey, no matter how small.
- I release all negative beliefs about my body and embrace self-love throughout my weight loss journey.
- I am grateful for my body's ability to transform and adapt.
- I let go of emotional eating and choose healthy alternatives that nourish my body.
- I listen to my body's hunger signals and eat mindfully, stopping when I am satisfied.
- I enjoy the process of finding new, delicious, and healthy recipes that support my weight loss goals.
- I am supported on my weight loss journey by loved ones, professionals, and my inner strength.
- I trust my body's ability to find its natural and healthy weight.

- I release any limiting beliefs that hinder my progress toward weight loss.
- I am creating a new, empowering relationship with food that supports my weight loss goals.
- I am patient and loving with myself throughout my weight loss journey.
- My body is becoming leaner, toned, and fit with each healthy choice I make.
- I prioritize self-care to nourish my mind, body, and soul as I work towards my weight loss goals.
- I view exercise as an enjoyable and beneficial activity that contributes to my weight loss.
- I release any fear or resistance towards exercise and embrace it as an opportunity to support my health and weight loss goals.
- I am in control of my eating habits and choose foods that nourish and support my weight loss.
- I trust my body's wisdom and give it the nourishment it needs without excess.
- I release any guilt or shame associated with previous weight loss attempts and start fresh with a positive mindset.
- Each day, I make progress towards my weight loss goals, becoming healthier and stronger.
- I have the power to change my body and create the weight and shape that I desire.
- I am worthy of a healthy, strong, and vibrant body.

- I love and accept myself at every stage of my weight loss journey.
- I celebrate my body's accomplishments and reward myself with non-food-related treats for reaching milestones.

These affirmations are designed to support you on your weight loss journey and help you maintain a positive mindset. Repeat them daily with belief and conviction, and watch as they empower and motivate you to achieve your weight loss goals. Remember, your journey is unique, and every step forward is a step closer to a healthier, happier you.

Anti-Ageing

Here are some affirmations for anti-ageing:

- I am grateful for the gift of ageing and the wisdom it brings.
- I embrace the natural process of ageing with grace and acceptance.
- My age reflects the experiences, knowledge, and strength I have gained.
- I radiate timeless beauty and vitality at every stage of life.
- I take loving care of my body, nourishing it with healthy choices and self-care.

- I release any attachment to societal standards of youth and embrace my unique beauty.
- I am comfortable and confident in my skin, celebrating the journey of ageing.
- I choose thoughts and beliefs that support my youthful spirit and energy.
- I am worthy of love, joy, and fulfillment at every age.
- I am ageless, as my true essence transcends physical appearances.
- I maintain a positive mindset, focusing on the present moment and the blessings of each day.
- I am grateful for the lines on my face, as they tell the story of a life well lived.
- My inner beauty shines through, illuminating my outer appearance.
- I nourish my body with healthy foods, exercise, and rest, supporting my overall well-being.
- I honour my body's wisdom and listen to its needs for optimal health and vibrancy.
- I practice self-compassion and self-love, embracing and accepting myself unconditionally.
- I am surrounded by positive energy and loving relationships that uplift and inspire me.
- I embrace change and growth, seeing each day as an opportunity for personal transformation.
- I am grateful for the support of loved ones and the wisdom shared among generations.

- I radiate joy, laughter, and happiness, which contribute to my youthful spirit.
- I let go of societal pressures and expectations, embracing my unique journey and path.
- I celebrate the beauty that comes with age, appreciating the uniqueness of my individuality.
- I prioritize self-care and make time for activities that bring me joy and enhance my well-being.
- I practice gratitude for my body, its resilience, and its ability to adapt to the changes of ageing.
- I am mindful of my thoughts and choose to focus on positivity and self-affirmation.
- I engage in activities that stimulate my mind, keeping it sharp and agile as I age.
- I am ageless in spirit, radiating a youthful energy that captivates and inspires others.
- I release any fear or worry about ageing, trusting in the beauty and wisdom that it brings.
- I am confident and comfortable in my skin, embracing my unique beauty.
- I am a beacon of light and inspiration, shining brightly regardless of my age.

These affirmations are designed to support you in embracing the process of ageing with love, acceptance, and a positive mindset. Repeat them daily with intention and belief, and watch as they help to shift your perspective and enhance your overall well-being. Remember, true beauty and vibrancy come from within, and as you embrace the gift of ageing, you radiate joy, confidence, and timeless grace.

Weight Gain

Here are some affirmations for weight gain:

- I am grateful for my body's ability to change and adapt.
- I embrace and accept my body at every stage, including times of weight gain.
- My worth and value are not determined by my weight or appearance.
- I nourish my body with love, respect, and healthy choices.
- I trust my body's wisdom in finding its natural and healthy weight.
- I release any guilt or shame associated with weight gain and focus on overall well-being.
- I am deserving of self-care and compassion, regardless of my size or shape.
- I am confident and comfortable in my body, knowing that true beauty comes from within.
- I am grateful for the strength and resilience of my body, regardless of its size.
- I am worthy of love and acceptance, regardless of changes in my weight.
- I let go of comparison and embrace my unique journey and body type.

- I celebrate and appreciate how my body serves me, including storing energy as weight.
- I choose thoughts and beliefs that empower and uplift me, focusing on my overall health and happiness.
- I listen to my body's needs and provide it with nourishment and care.
- I release any negative body image thoughts and replace them with positive affirmations.
- I am kind and gentle with myself, recognizing that my worth extends far beyond external appearances.
- I trust that my body knows what is best for me and will find its natural balance.
- I focus on the qualities and characteristics that make me unique and special, rather than my weight.
- I am grateful for the journey of self-discovery and growth that comes with changes in my body.
- I practice self-compassion and embrace self-love throughout my weight gain journey.
- I surround myself with positive influences and supportive individuals who celebrate me for who I am, not my weight.
- I release any attachment to societal standards of beauty and embrace my definition of beauty and worth.

- I nourish my body with healthy, nourishing foods that support my overall well-being.
- I release any negative judgments or criticisms about my body and replace them with affirmations of love and acceptance.
- I am grateful for the opportunity to learn and grow through the experience of weight gain.
- I honour and respect my body's unique journey, trusting that it knows what is best for me.
- I focus on the joy and happiness that comes from living a balanced and fulfilling life, rather than solely on my weight.
- I appreciate the lessons and insights that come from times of weight gain, allowing them to shape me into a stronger and more compassionate individual.
- I am patient and gentle with myself, knowing that change takes time and progress is a journey.
- I celebrate my body's resilience and capacity to adapt, knowing that it can find balance and well-being.

These affirmations are designed to support you in embracing the journey of weight gain with love, acceptance, and self-compassion. Repeat them daily with belief and conviction, and watch as they help shift your mindset to one of self-love and appreciation. Remember, your worth and value go beyond the number on the scale, and by focusing on overall well-being and self-care, you can embrace your body's natural journey and find joy in the process.

Healthy Hair

Affirmations can be beneficial for promoting healthy hair by influencing your mindset, reducing stress, and fostering a positive self-image.

Here are some of the examples of affirmations for healthy hair:

- I am proud of my hair, and I nurture it with love and gratitude.
- My hair is a symbol of my self-expression and individuality.
- Each day, my hair becomes more vibrant, healthy, and beautiful.
- I am blessed with strong, thick, and luxurious hair.
- I attract positive energy and compliments through the radiance of my hair.
- My hair reflects my inner vitality and well-being.
- I take pride in maintaining and caring for my beautiful hair.
- Every strand of my hair is filled with strength, vitality, and natural beauty.
- My hair is healthy, vibrant, and full of life.
- I am grateful for my luscious and beautiful hair.

- Every strand of my hair is strong and resilient.
- I radiate confidence and beauty through my gorgeous hair.
- I attract compliments about my stunning hair wherever I go.
- My hair reflects my inner beauty and vitality.
- I embrace and love every unique characteristic of my hair.
- My hair is a crown of natural beauty that sets me apart.
- I take excellent care of my hair, nourishing it with love and attention.
- I am blessed with beautiful hair that turns heads and catches attention.
- My hair reflects my overall well-being and self-care.
- I am deserving of healthy and fabulous hair.
- Each day, my hair becomes more abundant and gorgeous.
- I am grateful for the versatility and diversity of my hair.
- My hair effortlessly complements my style and enhances my overall appearance.
- I am connected to the natural beauty and power of my hair.
- My hair reflects my inner strength, resilience, and confidence.
- I embrace my hair's natural texture and celebrate its unique beauty.

- My hair is a canvas for creativity, and I enjoy experimenting with different hairstyles.
- I am in tune with my hair's needs and provide it with the care it requires.
- My hair grows abundantly, and I cherish every inch of its growth.

These affirmations are designed to help you affirm and celebrate the beauty of your hair. Repeat them daily with conviction and watch as your hair becomes even more radiant and beautiful. Embrace and appreciate the unique characteristics of your hair, and let it be a source of confidence and pride. While affirmations alone may not be a cure for specific hair issues, they can complement a holistic approach to health and wellness.

It is important to combine affirmations with a healthy lifestyle, proper nutrition, and good hair care practices for the best results. Once you are affirming for your good health, then you will go for abundance, success, and wealth affirmations. I know while reading this book, you will get the habit of repeating these affirmations in routine that is sufficient to change your thought pattern and once that purpose will achieve then you can change your reality. Let us be ready to see your new version in new year.

New Thoughts... New You

Chapter 8

Affirmations for Wealth & Success

"Affirmations are the oxygen for the soul. Breathe them in daily to rejuvenate your spirit." - Kelly Bouchard

Wealth affirmations are just one aspect of manifesting abundance. It is also important to act towards your financial goals, have a positive mindset and be open to receiving abundance in all areas of your life. Additionally, it's good to remember that manifesting abundance is not just about money, it is about feeling fulfilled, happy, and living a good life.

Wealth affirmations are positive statements or declarations that are consciously repeated to shape and influence our mindset regarding wealth, success, and abundance. These affirmations operate on the fundamental principle that our thoughts have the power to shape our reality. By consistently affirming positive beliefs about wealth, individuals aim to reprogram their subconscious mind, aligning it with the energy of prosperity and financial success.

If you want to increase your wealth and prosperity, one powerful thing you can do is start incorporating affirmations into your daily life. Affirmations are more than just saying the words aloud.

You must feel them. Lean into the sensation of immense wealth and prosperity.

How might that manifest in your life?

Consider the thoughts that serve you, empower you, and strengthen you. Here are some examples of Wealth Affirmations:

- I am a magnet for financial prosperity.
- Money flows effortlessly into my life.
- I attract abundance with every breath I take.
- My wealth reflects the value I provide to the world.
- I am open to receiving endless financial opportunities.
- I trust in my ability to create wealth.
- I deserve to be financially successful.
- I release all limiting beliefs about money.
- My financial success is a natural outcome of my positive mindset.
- I am in control of my financial destiny.
- Abundance is my birthright.
- I see opportunities for prosperity everywhere.

- The universe is conspiring to make me wealthy.
- I am grateful for the abundance present in my life.
- I attract prosperity with every thought, I think.
- I am worthy of abundance and wealth.
- I am open to receiving abundance and wealth in all areas of my life.
- I am grateful for all the abundance and wealth that flows into my life.
- I trust the Universe to provide for me in abundance.
- I am a money magnet, attracting abundance and wealth to me effortlessly.
- Wealth will provide the ability for me to be generous.
- My prosperity is limitless.
- I accept financial miracles.
- Financial blessings are coming my way.

Affirmations for Success

- I am achieving success in all areas of my life.
- Success is my natural state of being.
- I am worthy of the success that comes my way.
- Every challenge I face is an opportunity to grow and succeed.
- I am the architect of my success.
- I excel in my career, and success follows me.
- I am an asset to my workplace.

- I attract opportunities leading to career advancement.
- My work is recognized and rewarded generously.
- Success is drawn to me like a magnet.
- I trust in my ability to achieve my goals.
- I am confident in my capacity to succeed.
- Every setback is a setup for a greater comeback.
- I am determined to overcome all obstacles in my path.
- My success is inevitable.

Affirmations for Abundance

- I am grateful for the abundance that surrounds me.
- My life is filled with an abundance of love, joy, and prosperity.
- Abundance is a state of mind, and I choose to embody it.
- I celebrate the success and abundance of others.
- The more I give, the more I receive.
- I am grateful for the health and vitality that sustains me.
- Abundance extends to every aspect of my well-being.
- I attract positive energy that contributes to my health.

- Every day, I am becoming healthier and more vibrant.
- My body is a temple of abundance.
- I attract positive and fulfilling relationships to my life.
- My relationships are a source of joy and abundance.
- I am surrounded by love and support.
- I contribute positively to the lives of those around me.
- The more I give to my relationships, the more abundance I receive.

So, be specific about the wealth you want to attract. Believe in the affirmations. And reinforce the affirmations with actions. Positive affirmations when repeated and believed can rewire the subconscious mind. You may have unknowingly been self-sabotaging which was preventing you from attracting abundance. First, have a solid vision of what you desire. Do you want $2000 a month? Do you want to make over six figures a year? Or, do you want to win the lottery? This is where it gets tricky.

Staying home every day and avoiding working will not attract abundance or wealth no matter how many positive affirmations you say. You must align your life with your desires.

You can shift from a scarcity mindset to an abundance mindset by repeating positive affirmations. Repeating affirmations is a powerful way to transform your mindset. For that, you need to create a daily habit of consciously choosing your thoughts because when you change your thoughts, you can change your reality. You already have everything you need to be successful. You just need to believe in it.

Set a goal to create more abundance in an area of your life. Then, choose one or two affirmations from this list. Each day, write your affirmation in your journal 12 times, then, say it out loud. You could also write it on a sticky note and put it somewhere you will see it each day, or add it to your phone reminders to pop up at a certain time every day. The more you repeat positive affirmations, the more it reinforces a pattern of positive thinking. Over time, instead of defaulting to negative thoughts, you will naturally start to think more abundantly.

Affirmations are only the beginning.

Chapter 9

Affirmations for Love and Relationships

"Affirmations are the secret agents of the mind, that help us to rewrite the script of our lives." -Ravinder Kaur

Love is the most beautiful emotion in human life. We all want to receive love from loving people. Sometimes it's hard for us when we are ignored and rejected by that loving person. Right? That is why we need to create some positive and powerful thoughts within ourselves. It helps us to stay calm and quiet. The American author **Helen Keller** once said, *"The best and most beautiful things in the world cannot be seen or even touched. They must be felt with the heart."*

Yes, love is that emotion you cannot see or touch; but you can feel it in your heart. However, it would be best if you learned how to care for your loving emotions for the rest of your life. Also, you should learn how to care for those who love you most. It could be your parents, friends, and life partner.

3 Things to Consider While Writing Love Affirmations

If you want to write or make some love affirmations by yourself; then you should consider three things before it. These can help make some positive and powerful thoughts that you can affirm daily.

- **Simple Thoughts:** Try to make your statements so simple and easy to memorize that you can recite them on daily affirmations.

- **Positive & Powerful Words:** Make a list of positive and powerful words and use those words in your affirmation statements.

- **Using Present Tense:** While writing these affirmation statements; try to use the present moment so that you can feel those things happening right now.

- My love is unconditional.
- I will never give up on love.
- My partner reflects me.
- I take responsibility for my words and actions.
- I feel safe and protected by my partner.
- I am worthy of love.
- I deserve to find love.
- I believe in myself.
- I am surrounded by an abundance of love.

- My heart is open to letting someone's love come in.
- I happily give and receive love each day.
- I am making room for an amazing partner in my life.
- My partner shows me deep, passionate love.
- I forgive myself for things I have done wrong.
- I am so thankful for my partner.

Affirmations for Family, Friendship & Parents

The importance of family, friendship, and positive affirmations in the realm of personal growth and well-being cannot be overstated. These three pillars play a crucial role in shaping our lives, providing a foundation for emotional support, personal development, and overall happiness.

Affirmations for Family

Family is frequently regarded as the foundation of our existence. We first experience love, learn important values, and lay the foundation for our identity within the embrace of our families. Family gives us a sense of belonging and security, creating a nurturing environment in which we can discover our potential and face life's challenges. Family affirmations emphasize the significance of these bonds. Affirmative statements like "My family is a source of strength and support in my life" and "I am committed to creating a loving and nurturing home for my family" highlight the positive impact of family relationships on our emotional well-being.

- My relationship with my family is strong and built on trust and love.
- I am grateful for all the members of my family.
- I love my family and they love me.
- My family deserves happiness.
- We build each other up.
- We celebrate each other's happiness and successes.
- Our joy inspires other families to be happy as well.
- I like spending time with my family.
- I share a healthy relationship with each member of my family.
- My family is my support system.
- I feel understood by my family.
- I feel loved by my family.
- I am grateful for my family.
- It is easy for me to be myself with my family.
- I love my family unconditionally.
- I feel grateful to be a part of such a beautiful family.
- I listen to my family's needs.
- I always look to understand my family.
- I feel grateful for my family at this moment.

- I enjoy being with my family.

Affirmations for Friendship

Friendship affirmations emphasize the importance of building and keeping these significant friendships. Statements such as "I am a good friend, and I deserve strong, meaningful connections" and "I am surrounded by friends who inspire and motivate me to reach my potential" support the view that friendships contribute to our personal growth and provide a support system outside of the familial arena.

- I attract positive and genuine friends into my life.
- My friendships are built on trust, mutual respect, and understanding.
- I am grateful for the supportive and uplifting friends in my life.
- I am a good friend, and I deserve strong, meaningful connections.
- I surround myself with friends who inspire and encourage me to be my best self.
- I am open to forming new friendships.
- My friendships bring joy, laughter, and shared experiences into my life.
- I appreciate the diversity of personalities and perspectives within my friend circle.

- I am a loyal and dependable friend, and my friends value my presence in their lives.
- I let go of toxic friendships and make room for positive, nurturing connections.
- I communicate openly and honestly with my friends, fostering deep connections.
- I am a good listener, and I provide support to my friends when they need it.
- I celebrate the successes and milestones of my friends with genuine happiness.
- I attract friends who share similar values and goals, creating a harmonious bond.
- My friendships are a source of comfort, understanding, and shared growth.
- I am surrounded by friends who appreciate and accept me for who I am.
- I contribute positively to the lives of my friends, and they enhance mine in return.
- I forgive and let go of any misunderstandings, nurturing healthy friendships.
- My social circle is filled with friends who inspire and motivate me to reach my potential.
- I am a magnet for authentic and lasting friendships.

Affirmations for Parents

As the architects of our early experiences, our parents have a huge impact on our perspective and beliefs. Affirmations for parents acknowledge their importance in our lives and affirm our dedication to strong familial ties. We actively contribute to a healthy family dynamic by acknowledging ourselves as caring and nurturing parents or showing trust in our parenting intuition. These affirmations serve as a gentle reminder that the parent-child relationship is an ongoing process of learning, growth, and mutual support.

- I am a loving and nurturing parent.
- I am doing my best, and that is always enough.
- My child is a gift, and I cherish every moment with them.
- I am patient and understanding in my role as a parent.
- I lead by example, teaching valuable life lessons to my child.
- My love and support create a secure and stable environment for my family.
- I am present and engaged in my child's life, fostering a strong connection.
- I trust my instincts and make decisions that are in the best interest of my family.
- I am open to learning and growing as a parent every day.
- I celebrate the unique qualities and talents of each of my children.
- My home is filled with love, laughter, and positive energy.

- I communicate with my children with kindness and respect.
- I forgive myself for any parenting mistakes and use them as opportunities for growth.
- I am a role model for resilience and perseverance in the face of challenges.
- I encourage my children to express themselves and embrace their individuality.
- I create a balance between nurturing and allowing independence in my child.
- I take care of my well-being so that I can be the best parent for my family.
- I appreciate the joy and beauty that my children bring into my life.
- I am a source of comfort and support for my children in times of need.
- I am proud of the positive impact I have had on my children's lives.

Affirmations are deliberate declarations of our values that influence our mentality and actions. Friendships enrich our path by sharing shared experiences, and positive affirmations serve as guiding principles, boosting gratitude and resilience. These factors weave a tapestry of meaningful connections and personal progress, all of which contribute to a full and purposeful existence.

Chapter 10

Affirmations for Self-Image

"Believe you can and you're halfway there." - Theodore Roosevelt

Affirmations can help increase your confidence. If you believe that it works for you. But if you don't believe it, then it won't work for you. By doing daily affirmation practice, your confidence level will increase. The American business author and international best-selling author **Robert Kiyosaki** said, *"Confidence comes from discipline and training."* You can build your confidence by practising and training yourself. You can read the world's best self-help books, read affirmation books, watch TED Talks videos, listen to podcasts and do affirmations to enhance your self-confidence and self-worth. You can write your statements for affirming yourself. Before writing affirmations, you need three things to consider most. When I wrote my own, I followed those things.

- **Write it Simple:** Where are you right now? What was the biggest fear at this moment? You know better yourself. Try to think from all perspectives and write those statements simply so that you can get to heart easily.

- **Use positive and powerful words:** While you write your statements, use some positive and powerful words that can help uplift and boost your confidence. Also, you can write some statements that start with "I AM." This is the best for start your affirmations.

- **Use present tense:** Mostly I want to suggest you, use the present tense while you write your positive thoughts. Because, when you recite those statements, you can feel the present moment. And it helps to get back your self-confidence.

After finishing your writing affirmations, it is time to practice regularly.

Self-Confidence

Self-confidence is the belief and assurance in one's abilities, qualities, and judgment. It is an internal attitude that reflects an individual's trust in their capacity to achieve goals, overcome challenges, and navigate life's uncertainties. Self-confidence is not a fixed trait but a dynamic quality that can be cultivated and strengthened over time through positive experiences and self-affirmation.

Self-confidence is a cornerstone of psychological well-being and personal development. Its importance extends across various aspects of life, influencing behaviour, decision-making, relationships, and overall life satisfaction. Here are several key reasons highlighting the significance of self-confidence:

- **Positive Self-Image**: Self-confidence contributes to a positive self-image. When individuals believe in their abilities and worth, they are more likely to view themselves in a favourable light. This positive self-image lays the foundation for mental and emotional well-being.

- **Motivation and Goal Achievement:** Self-confident individuals are motivated to set and pursue goals. The belief in one's capabilities serves as a driving force, propelling individuals to take on challenges and persevere in the face of obstacles. Self-confidence is a catalyst for goal achievement and personal success.

- **Resilience in the Face of Challenges**: Challenges and setbacks are inevitable in life. Self-confidence acts as a buffer, helping individuals bounce back from failures and adversity. A confident mindset enables resilience, allowing individuals to view challenges as opportunities for growth rather than insurmountable obstacles.

- **Effective Communication:** Self-confidence enhances communication skills. Individuals who believe in themselves are more likely to express their thoughts, ideas, and opinions with clarity and conviction. Effective communication, in turn, fosters positive interactions in personal and professional relationships.

- **Healthy Relationships:** Self-confidence is a crucial factor in building and maintaining healthy relationships. Confident individuals are better equipped to assert boundaries, express needs, and engage in open communication. This contributes to the development of strong and mutually supportive connections with others.

- **Decision-Making Abilities:** Confident individuals trust their judgment and decision-making abilities. They are more likely to make informed choices, take calculated risks, and navigate uncertainty with a sense of self-assurance. This enhances the overall quality of decision-making in various life domains.

- **Career Success:** In the professional realm, self-confidence is linked to career success. Confident individuals are more likely to pursue challenging opportunities, showcase their skills, and seek advancement. A confident demeanour can positively influence colleagues and employers, contributing to career growth.

- **Emotional Well-Being:** Self-confidence is closely tied to emotional well-being. Confident individuals experience lower levels of anxiety and self-doubt, leading to a greater overall sense of happiness and contentment. Positive self-esteem, nurtured by self-confidence, is a cornerstone of emotional resilience.

- **Adaptability and Openness to Learning:** Confidence fosters adaptability and a willingness to learn. Confident individuals are open to new experiences, receptive to feedback, and resilient in the face of change. This adaptability contributes to personal growth and a broader perspective on life.

- **Assertiveness:** Assertiveness is a key aspect of self-confidence. Confident individuals can assert their needs, express opinions, and respectfully advocate for themselves. This assertiveness is essential for maintaining self-respect and fostering positive relationships.

Affirmations for Building Self-Confidence

Affirmations are positive statements that, when repeated consistently, can reshape thought patterns and reinforce a positive mindset. Incorporating self-confidence affirmations into daily life is a proactive way to cultivate and strengthen this essential quality. Recite your affirmation for boosting your self-confidence.

- Confidence is my second nature.
- I am energetic and enthusiastic.
- People love my confidence
- I am flexible I adapt to change quickly.
- I am purely confident in all situations.
- I always exude the vibration of confidence.
- I believe things will always work out for me.
- It is extremely easy for me to make friends.
- I attract positive and kind people into my life.
- I attract unlimited opportunities because of my confidence.
- I can hold a wonderful conversation with any nationality in any culture.
- I believe and love myself.
- I can stand up to anything.
- I meet new people with ease.
- I speak out with confidence.
- My personality always shines forth.
- I am confident.
- I take action daily.
- I have overcome shyness.
- I face my life head-on daily.
- I have full trust in myself.

- I am 100% confident in myself.
- My confidence is increasing.
- I face anything that confronts me.
- I easily overcome any failures.
- I am confident in my abilities and believe in myself.
- I trust my judgment and decisions.
- Confidence is my natural state of being.
- I am motivated to pursue my goals with passion and determination.
- I have the power to overcome any challenges that come my way.
- My confidence propels me toward success.
- I bounce back from setbacks stronger than before.
- Challenges are growth opportunities, and I embrace them with confidence.
- I believe in my ability to navigate life's uncertainties.
- I communicate with clarity and confidence.
- My opinions and ideas are valuable, and I express them with assurance.
- Confident communication fosters positive connections with others.
- I am deserving of healthy and supportive relationships.
- I assert my boundaries with confidence, nurturing positive connections.

- Confidence enhances the quality of my relationships.
- I trust my intuition and make decisions with confidence.
- Every decision I make contributes to my growth and well-being.
- Confidence guides me in making wise and informed choices.
- I am confident in my professional abilities and seek growth opportunities.
- Confidence opens doors to success and advancement in my career.
- I showcase my skills and talents with confidence in the workplace.
- I release self-doubt and embrace a confident and positive mindset.
- My confidence contributes to my overall sense of happiness and contentment.
- I am resilient in the face of challenges, thanks to my confidence.
- I am open to new experiences and opportunities for learning.
- Confidence allows me to adapt to change with grace and resilience.
- Every new experience is a chance for personal growth, and I face it with confidence.
- I assert my needs and express my opinions with confidence and respect.

- Confidence empowers me to advocate for myself and maintain self-respect.
- I am assertive and confident in all my interactions.

Recognizing the importance of self-confidence in various aspects of life prompts an understanding of its positive impact on motivation, resilience, relationships, and overall satisfaction. Affirmations, when integrated into daily life, serve as powerful tools for building and reinforcing self-confidence.

By actively cultivating a confident mindset through positive affirmations, individuals can enhance their belief in themselves, unlock their potential, and navigate life with a sense of assurance and empowerment.

Attitude

Attitude is a mental and emotional disposition that shapes how individuals perceive and respond to the world around them. It encompasses beliefs, feelings, and behavioural tendencies that influence one's approach to situations, people, and life in general. Attitude is not only a reflection of personal values but also a powerful force that can significantly impact one's experiences and interactions. The significance of attitude in life cannot be overstated. It shapes perceptions, influences behaviour, and ultimately determines the quality of one's experiences. Here are several key reasons why attitude is of utmost importance:

- **Impact on Relationships:** Attitude plays a pivotal role in interpersonal dynamics. A positive attitude fosters healthy and supportive relationships, while a negative one can strain connections and hinder effective communication. Cultivating a positive attitude contributes to harmonious interactions with family, friends, and colleagues.

- **Achieving Goals:** Attitude significantly influences goal-setting and achievement. A positive attitude fuels motivation, resilience, and a proactive approach to challenges. Individuals with a constructive attitude are more likely to persevere, learn from setbacks, and ultimately reach their objectives.

- **Emotional Well-being:** Attitude directly affects emotional well-being. Maintaining a positive attitude contributes to lower stress levels, enhanced emotional resilience, and improved mental health. It empowers individuals to navigate life's ups and downs with a greater sense of balance and composure.

- **Professional Success:** In the workplace, attitude is a key factor in professional success. Employers value employees with positive attitudes who contribute to a collaborative and productive work environment. A positive attitude fosters creativity, problem-solving skills, and adaptability, crucial attributes for career advancement.

- **Health and Well-being:** Numerous studies highlight the connection between attitude and physical health. A positive attitude is associated with better health outcomes, improved immune function, and a reduced risk of chronic diseases. It emphasizes the mind-body connection, highlighting the impact of mental states on overall well-being.

- **Adaptability and Resilience:** Life is filled with uncertainties and challenges. A positive attitude enhances adaptability and resilience, enabling individuals to navigate change with a more open and optimistic mindset. This adaptability is crucial for personal growth and overcoming obstacles.

- **Influence on Perception:** Attitude shapes how individuals perceive the world. A positive attitude allows for a more optimistic interpretation of events, while a negative attitude may lead to distorted perceptions and a focus on shortcomings. The lens through which one views the world significantly impacts the overall life experience.

Affirmations for Cultivating a Positive Attitude

Affirmations are powerful tools for shaping and reinforcing attitudes. They are positive statements that, when repeated consistently, influence thought patterns and contribute to the development of a constructive mindset. Here are affirmations tailored to cultivating a positive attitude:

- I am grateful for the blessings in my life.
- I appreciate the positive aspects of each day.
- Gratitude opens my heart to joy and abundance.
- I choose optimism and positivity in all situations.
- Every challenge is an opportunity for growth.
- My optimistic outlook shapes a brighter future.
- I believe in my abilities and potential.
- I can overcome any obstacles.
- My self-confidence empowers me to succeed.
- I bounce back from setbacks stronger than before.
- Challenges are opportunities for resilience and learning.
- I embrace difficulties with a resilient spirit.

- I am open to new ideas and perspectives.
- Every experience is a learning opportunity.
- Open-mindedness enriches my life.
- I choose positivity over negativity.
- Positive thoughts create a positive reality.
- My attitude shapes the energy I bring into the world.
- I am present in each moment, appreciating life.
- Mindfulness enhances my awareness and clarity.
- I cultivate peace by staying present.
- I radiate kindness and compassion.
- Acts of kindness contribute to a positive world.
- Kindness reflects my positive attitude.
- I embrace change with a flexible and adaptable mindset.
- Adaptability is my strength in navigating life's journey.
- Change brings new growth opportunities.
- I love and accept myself unconditionally.
- Self-love is the foundation of a positive attitude.
- I treat myself with kindness and compassion.

A positive attitude contributes to healthy relationships, goal achievement, emotional well-being, professional success, and overall life satisfaction. Affirmations, as powerful tools, assist in cultivating and reinforcing a positive mindset, fostering resilience, adaptability, and a more optimistic approach to life's challenges.

Recognizing the impact of attitude and incorporating positive affirmations into daily life can lead to a transformative and fulfilling journey towards personal growth and well-being.

Memory

Memory is the cognitive function that allows individuals to encode, store, and retrieve information from past experiences. It involves the complex processes of acquiring, retaining, and recalling knowledge, events, or skills. Memory is a fundamental aspect of human cognition, influencing learning, decision-making, and overall mental functioning.

Importance of Memory

Memory plays a central role in various aspects of life, influencing cognitive functions, academic performance, daily activities, and overall well-being. Here are several key reasons highlighting the importance of memory:

- **Learning and Education:** Memory is fundamental to the learning process. It allows individuals to acquire and retain knowledge, recall facts, and apply information in academic settings. Strong memory enhances comprehension, critical thinking, and problem-solving skills.

- **Decision-Making:** Memory influences decision-making by providing a basis for evaluating past experiences and outcomes. The ability to recall previous decisions and their consequences enables individuals to make informed choices and avoid repeating mistakes.

- **Daily Functioning**: Memory is crucial for daily activities, ranging from remembering appointments and tasks to recalling names and faces. It facilitates effective communication and the execution of routine tasks, contributing to overall efficiency and organization.

- **Personal and Cultural Identity:** Memory shapes personal identity by preserving experiences that define individuals. It also plays a role in cultural identity, as shared memories contribute to a collective sense of history and heritage within communities.

- **Emotional Well-being:** Memory is intertwined with emotional experiences. Positive memories contribute to a sense of happiness and fulfillment, while negative memories can inform personal growth and resilience. The ability to recall positive experiences enhances emotional well-being.

- **Professional Success**: In professional settings, memory is crucial for retaining and applying job-related information. It influences productivity, problem-solving abilities, and the development of expertise in various fields, contributing to career success.

- **Adaptability:** Memory aids in adapting to new situations by drawing on past experiences. The ability to recall solutions to similar challenges enhances adaptability and the capacity to navigate novel circumstances effectively.

- **Relationships:** Memory plays a pivotal role in relationships by preserving shared experiences and fostering emotional connections. Remembering important events, anniversaries, and details about loved ones strengthens the bonds between individuals.

- **Creativity:** Memory is an integral component of creativity. It allows individuals to draw on a reservoir of knowledge and experiences, combining elements in novel ways. Creative endeavours often involve the synthesis of remembered information.

- **Health and Safety:** Memory is essential for maintaining health and safety. It enables individuals to remember medication schedules, follow medical advice, and recall safety procedures. Memory lapses can have implications for both physical and mental well-being.

Affirmations for Enhancing Memory

Affirmations can serve as effective tools for enhancing memory by promoting positive beliefs and reinforcing the mindset conducive to optimal cognitive function. Here are affirmations tailored to support memory improvement:

- My memory is sharp and reliable.
- I easily absorb and retain new information.
- Remembering details comes naturally to me.
- I am a capable learner, and my memory serves me well in academic pursuits.
- Retaining information is easy for me, and I excel in my studies.
- I approach learning with a focused and receptive mind.
- My memory guides me in making wise and informed decisions.
- I trust my ability to recall relevant information when faced with choices.
- Reflecting on past experiences enhances my decision-making skills.
- I effortlessly remember and execute my daily tasks with efficiency.
- Recalling names, dates, and details is a natural part of my daily life.

- My memory supports my organizational skills and overall productivity.
- My memory is an asset in my professional endeavours.
- I easily recall and apply relevant information in my work.
- Continuous learning and a sharp memory contribute to my career success.
- My memory helps me adapt to new situations with ease.
- Recalling past solutions empowers me to navigate challenges effectively.
- Adaptability is a natural outcome of my sharp memory.
- I cherish and remember the special moments in my relationships.
- My memory deepens the emotional connections I share with others.
- Remembering important details strengthens my relationships.
- My memory is a wellspring of ideas and creative inspiration.
- Recalling diverse experiences fuels my creative endeavours.
- I easily draw upon my memory to innovate and think outside the box.
- I remember and follow health guidelines for my well-being.

- Safety procedures are ingrained in my memory, ensuring my protection.
- My memory supports my overall health and safety.

Recognizing the importance of memory prompts an understanding of its role in shaping personal and collective experiences. Affirmations, when integrated into daily life, can serve as powerful tools for enhancing memory, fostering a positive mindset, and contributing to cognitive well-being. Individuals can actively support and optimize their mental function, leading to a more enriched and fulfilling life by incorporating affirmations into their routines.

Chapter 11

Affirmations for Forgiveness and Peace

"I forgive others not because they deserve forgiveness, but because I deserve peace."

-

Ravinder Kaur

Forgiveness is the act of releasing resentment and pardoning wrongdoing. It involves letting go of negative emotions and granting freedom from blame. Examples include forgiving a friend for a mistake, reconciling after a disagreement, or choosing to move forward without holding onto grudges for personal growth and well-being.

1. **Emotional Healing:** Forgiveness affirmations can assist you in releasing pent-up negative feelings and healing emotional wounds. You can experience emotional relief and make room for happy feelings by realizing your potential to forgive and let go of resentment.

2. **Reducing Stress:** Holding grudges and unsolved confrontations can contribute to persistent stress and anxiety. Affirmations of forgiveness can help

reduce stress by moving your emphasis from negativity to a more pleasant and tranquil mindset.

3. **Improved Relationships:** Relationships can be made better and more peaceful by speaking forgiveness affirmations. You can restore damaged ties, rebuild trust, and develop bonds with others by letting go of animosity and offering forgiveness.

4. **Self-Empowerment:** Forgiveness affirmations empower you by reminding you that forgiveness is a choice that you have control over. This sense of empowerment might assist you in regaining control of your emotions and reactions to challenging situations.

5. **Release of Negative Energy:** When you hold grudges, you carry negative energy with you, which can have an impact on your entire well-being. Forgiveness affirmations assist you in releasing bad energy and making room for positive, healing energy.

6. **Personal Development:** Forgiveness is a great tool for personal development and transformation. You can improve and mature as an individual by expressing your ability to forgive, learning from past experiences and moving forward with more wisdom.

7. **Cultivating Compassion:** Forgiveness affirmations can help you develop compassion for yourself as well as others. You can improve your self-compassion and self-esteem by practising self-forgiveness.

8. **Enhanced Mental Health:** Forgiveness is related to good mental health because it helps lower symptoms of melancholy, anxiety, and rage. Forgiveness affirmations can benefit your overall mental health.

9. **Forgiveness and Inner Serenity:** Forgiveness and inner serenity are inextricably linked. You attract a sense of calm and serenity into your life by reciting forgiveness affirmations, making it easier to manage difficult situations with grace.

10. **Positive Outlook:** Affirmations of forgiveness promote a more cheerful and optimistic attitude in life. They assist you in shifting your focus from lamenting the past to embracing the present and future with optimism.

Including forgiveness affirmations in your daily practice can be a significant step toward personal development, emotional healing, and living a more peaceful and fulfilled life. It is a discipline that promotes well-being for yourself as well as in your connections with others. Forgiveness is a powerful act of letting go and healing. Here are some affirmations to help you cultivate forgiveness in life:

- I release the burden of resentment and embrace the freedom that forgiveness brings.
- Forgiveness is my gift to myself, a key to unlocking inner peace and healing.
- I choose to forgive, not because others deserve it, but because I deserve peace.
- I am in control of my emotions, and I choose to let go of anger and bitterness.
- Forgiveness is the path to emotional liberation, and I walk this path with an open heart.
- I release the past, freeing myself to create a brighter future filled with love and compassion.
- By forgiving others, I set myself free from the chains of the past, and I reclaim my power.
- I am a source of love and understanding, and forgiveness flows through me effortlessly.
- Forgiveness is a strength, not a weakness, and I choose to be strong in the face of hurt.
- I am a beacon of forgiveness, illuminating the path to healing for myself and others.
- I let go of grudges and embrace the cleansing power of forgiveness, renewing my spirit.
- I am a work in progress, and forgiveness is a step toward my personal growth and transformation.
- Forgiveness is an act of self-love, and I love myself enough to forgive and move forward.

- I release the pain of the past and make room for the love and joy of the present.
- Every day, I choose forgiveness, and with each choice, I become lighter and more peaceful.

Affirmations for forgiveness can help you heal, find inner peace, and make room in your life for love and compassion. Regularly repeating these affirmations can be a powerful tool in your journey toward forgiveness.

Peace

Peace is of paramount importance to individuals, communities, nations, and the world. Its significance transcends cultural, geographical, and ideological boundaries, making it a fundamental and universal value. The importance of peace can be understood from various perspectives, including individual well-being, societal harmony, economic development, and global stability.

1. Individual Well-being: Peace is closely linked to mental well-being. In peaceful environments, individuals experience lower levels of stress, anxiety, and fear. The absence of conflict contributes to a sense of security and promotes mental health.

Peaceful surroundings create a conducive environment for individuals to lead fulfilling lives. People in peaceful communities are more likely to enjoy a higher quality of life with access to education, healthcare, and opportunities for personal growth.

2. Societal Harmony: Peace fosters social cohesion by promoting understanding, tolerance, and cooperation among diverse individuals and groups. It helps build a sense of community and shared identity, reducing the likelihood of social conflicts.

Peace is essential for the establishment of just and equitable societies. In the absence of violence and unrest, there is a greater opportunity to address social injustices, discrimination, and inequality.

3. Economic Development: Peaceful environments attract investments and promote economic growth. Businesses thrive in stable conditions, and nations engaged in peaceful relationships are more likely to engage in international trade, contributing to economic development.

Nations at peace can allocate resources to infrastructure development, education, and research rather than military expenditures. This leads to increased innovation, technological advancements, and overall economic progress.

4. Global Stability: Peace is the foundation of international diplomacy and cooperation. Nations that prioritize peaceful resolutions over conflicts contribute to global stability. Multilateral cooperation is essential for addressing global challenges such as climate change, pandemics, and poverty.

Peace is crucial for addressing humanitarian issues. In times of conflict, civilians often bear the brunt of the consequences, facing displacement, hunger, and loss of life. Peaceful conditions allow for the delivery of humanitarian aid and the protection of vulnerable populations.

5. Environmental Sustainability: Peace is intertwined with environmental sustainability. In regions affected by conflict, natural resources are often exploited without regard for environmental consequences. Peaceful coexistence allows for the preservation of ecosystems and biodiversity.

Global efforts to address climate change require collaboration and shared responsibility. Peaceful relations between nations facilitate joint initiatives to combat climate change and protect the planet for future generations.

6. Cultural and Artistic Flourishing: Peace encourages cultural exchange and the celebration of diversity. In peaceful times, people from different cultures can interact, share ideas, and appreciate each other's traditions, fostering a rich tapestry of global cultural heritage.

Peaceful environments provide the freedom for artistic expression. Artists, writers, and musicians can flourish and contribute to the cultural richness of societies without fear of censorship or repression.

7. Interpersonal Relationships: Peace is the bedrock of healthy interpersonal relationships. Families, communities, and friendships thrive in peaceful environments, enabling individuals to build supportive networks and meaningful connections.

Peaceful societies encourage the use of dialogue and negotiation to resolve conflicts. Conflict resolution skills are essential for maintaining healthy relationships on both personal and societal levels.

8. Preservation of Heritage: Peace is essential for the preservation of cultural heritage and historical sites. During times of conflict, these invaluable aspects of human history are often at risk of destruction or damage.

Peace allows for the transmission of knowledge, traditions, and values from one generation to the next. It ensures that future generations can learn from the past and contribute to the ongoing development of societies.

Here are some peace affirmations for you to repeat daily:

- I effortlessly channel the elegance of tranquillity into my daily life, becoming a living embodiment of peace.
- In the symphony of existence, I am the conductor of calm, orchestrating a masterpiece of serenity.
- With every graceful step I take, I leave behind footprints of peace, creating a path of elegance and composure.
- I wear peace like a well-tailored suit, exuding sophistication and poise in every situation.
- In the art of living, I paint my canvas with the soothing hues of peace, creating a masterpiece of style and serenity.
- I am the epitome of grace under pressure, effortlessly maintaining a sense of tranquillity and refinement.
- "Peace flows through me like a fine wine, enhancing the flavours of life with a touch of sophistication and class."

- My presence exudes an aura of calm and grace, leaving an indelible mark of style and elegance on those I encounter.
- I am a connoisseur of inner peace, savouring its subtle nuances and displaying it with effortless chic.
- In a world of noise and chaos, I am the embodiment of timeless elegance, radiating the allure of peace.

These stylish affirmations infuse the concept of peace with a touch of sophistication and elegance, emphasizing the graceful and refined nature of inner serenity.

Life

Life is a complex, beautiful journey filled with joy, challenges, and growth opportunities. Every day is a new chapter in my life story. In this world, where every sunrise represents a new beginning, I recognize the profound value of life. I recognize that my very existence is a miracle in and of itself. This affirmation is a thank you for the gift of life that has been given to me.

I express my gratitude for each day, for the opportunity to witness the world's wonders, for the chance to connect with people, and for the ability to feel a wide range of emotions. Life is a priceless tapestry woven with laughter threads. I reaffirm my commitment to living intentionally. I recognize that life is more than a series of random events; it is a journey that I can shape and mould. Setting clear intentions allows me to guide my actions, choices, and decisions in ways that are consistent with my values and aspirations.

In the face of adversity, I affirm my resilience. Life is not without its challenges, but I believe that adversity can be a powerful catalyst for personal development. I am capable and strong, and I have the inner strength to overcome challenges with grace and determination.

I repeat my dedication to self-care. I treasure both the gift of life and the vessel that carries me through it: my body and mind. I promise to nourish them with love, compassion, and care, knowing that a healthy body and a peaceful mind are necessary for a happy life.

I reiterate my commitment to lifelong learning and development. Life is an ever-changing adventure, and I am dedicated to broadening my knowledge, honing my skills, and broadening my horizons. I view change as an opportunity for personal growth and transformation. I confirm my bond with others. Life is not a solitary journey, but rather a shared experience. I cherish the relationships I have with family, friends, and the broader community. I am committed to nurturing these connections, offering support, and receiving it in return.

I declare my commitment to the world around me. I am aware that my actions affect the environment, society, and future generations. I am committed to making environmentally sustainable, socially responsible, and ethical decisions. I reaffirm my desire for happiness. Life is about more than just surviving; it is about thriving. I vow to seek out happy moments, to savour small pleasures, and to cultivate a sense of contentment that pervades my life.

I declare my unwavering commitment to living a life of gratitude, intention, resilience, self-care, growth, connection, responsibility, and happiness in this life affirmation. I recognize that life is a journey with ups and downs, and I am ready to embrace it in all its complexities. With an open heart and a positive spirit, I step forward into each new day, ready to seize the opportunities it presents and to make the most of this incredible gift we call life.

Chapter 12

Inspirational Stories

Some people credit affirmations for bringing about positive changes in their lives when used consistently and with belief. Here are a few examples of people who have shared their stories about how affirmations have helped them:

1. **Louise Hay:** Louise Hay, a renowned motivational author and speaker and founder of Hay House, is a prominent figure in the self-help and affirmations  movement. She emphasized the power of affirmations in her book "You Can Heal Your Life." Louise Hay used affirmations to overcome personal challenges and went on to inspire millions with her positive philosophy. Louise Hay's teachings have inspired many to adopt positive affirmations for self-improvement.

2. **Oprah Winfrey:** Oprah Winfrey, one of the most influential media tycoons in the world, has spoken about the role of affirmations in her success. She is  known to have used affirmations to maintain a positive mindset and overcome obstacles

throughout her career. Oprah's journey from a challenging upbringing to becoming a media mogul and philanthropist is often attributed partly to her positive mindset. Oprah is known for her positive mindset and belief in the power of affirmations.

3. Jim Carrey: Actor and comedian Jim Carrey is famous for sharing his story of using affirmations to manifest his success. In the early 1990s, he wrote himself a check for 10  million dollars and dated it for five years in the future. He visualised and affirmed his success, eventually receiving a movie role that paid him exactly that amount. He claims that this practice, along with persistent hard work, played a role in his rise to stardom.

4. Will Smith: Will Smith, the acclaimed actor and producer, is known for his positive mindset and belief in the power of affirmations. He has spoken about using  affirmations to set goals and maintain focus throughout his career.

5. Ellen DeGeneres: Talk show host Ellen DeGeneres has mentioned the role of positive affirmations in her life. Despite facing challenges, including a public coming out in the late 1990s, she has used affirmations to stay true to herself and build a successful career. During difficult times in her career, Ellen affirmed her worth and talent, eventually achieving success. She has since used her  platform to spread joy and promote kindness and inclusivity.

6. Tony Robbins: Tony Robbins, a motivational speaker, and life coach, often emphasizes the importance of positive affirmations in his teachings. He  encourages people to use affirmations as a tool for personal growth and transformation. His teachings encourage individuals to adopt a positive mindset and use affirmations.

7. Mahatma Gandhi: Gandhi, the leader of the Indian independence movement, practised affirmations, and positive  thinking as part of his philosophy of nonviolent resistance. His commitment to his beliefs and affirmations played a crucial role in India's fight for independence.

8. Nick Vujicic: Nick Vujicic, born without limbs, is a motivational speaker and author who has inspired millions with his positive outlook on life. Nick often speaks about using affirmations to  overcome challenges and build a life filled with purpose and meaning.

9. Malala Yousafzai: Malala, a Pakistani activist for female education, survived an assassination attempt by the Taliban at a young age. Throughout her recovery and  subsequent advocacy work, Malala used affirmations to strengthen her resilience and commitment to education for all. Affirmations like "I am a voice for the voiceless." empowered her to become the youngest-ever Nobel Prize laureate, making a global impact on education rights. Malala Yousafzai stands as a symbol of courage and tenacity.

10. Steve Jobs: The late co-founder of Apple, Steve Jobs, was known for his visionary mindset and focus on  innovation. Jobs reportedly practised affirmations to maintain his sense of purpose and determination during challenging times. His famous affirmation was, "I am here to make a dent in the universe," reflecting his commitment to creating transformative technology.

11. J.K. Rowling: J.K.  Rowling, the author of the Harry Potter series, faced numerous rejections before finding success. During challenging times, Rowling used affirmations to maintain her belief in her writing abilities. She often affirmed, "I will succeed despite setbacks" and "My imagination knows no limits." Today, she is one of the most successful authors in the world.

12. Serena Williams:  Tennis champion Serena Williams is known for her mental resilience on the court. She has spoken about using affirmations to boost her confidence and focus. Affirmations like "I am a champion" and "I have the strength to overcome any challenge" have contributed to her remarkable career and numerous Grand Slam victories.

13. Michelle Obama: The former First Lady of the United States, Michelle Obama, has shared her journey of self-discovery and the importance of positive affirmations. Affirmations such as "I am enough" and "My voice matters" played a role in shaping her confidence and resilience, allowing her to make a significant impact on education, health, and military families.

14. Rosa Parks: Rosa Parks, often referred to as the "Mother of the Civil Rights Movement," used affirmations to fortify her courage during a pivotal moment in history. Parks affirmed her belief in equality and justice, contributing to her refusal to give up her seat on a segregated bus. Her actions sparked the Montgomery Bus Boycott, a significant event in the civil rights struggle.

15. Nelson Mandela: Nelson Mandela, the anti-apartheid revolutionary and former President of South Africa, relied on affirmations during his long imprisonment. Mandela affirmed beliefs in justice, equality, and forgiveness, which sustained him during challenging times. After his release, Mandela played a pivotal role in ending

discrimination and fostering settlement in South Africa.

16. Elon Musk: Elon Musk, the visionary entrepreneur behind companies like SpaceX and Tesla, has not only revolutionized industries but has also openly credited the  power of affirmations for steering him through challenges and setbacks. Musk's journey in the world of business and technology is characterized by audacious goals, and during moments of adversity, he turned to positive affirmations to reinforce his commitment to innovation and progress. He adopted a mindset that blended determination with a belief in the transformative power of affirmations. Affirmations such as "I will create revolutionary change" became more than mere motivational statements for Musk; they were guiding principles steering him toward his ambitious objectives.

17. Muniba Mazari: Muniba Mazari, a Pakistani artist, and a motivational speaker, is known for her inspiring story of resilience and determination after

surviving a life-changing accident. She is known for her positive and empowering messages. She focuses on embracing challenges, finding strength in adversity, and encouraging self-love. She believes life is a test, embrace failures but never give up.

"Some trials come to sort the life of people out. They break you, deform you, and then transform you into the best version of you. You are the hero of your own story; and heroes never give up."   -Muniba Mazari

These stories illustrate how individuals from diverse backgrounds and fields have used affirmations to navigate challenges, find strength, and contribute to positive change on a global scale. Affirmations can serve as powerful tools for personal growth and resilience, influencing both the individuals who practice them and the world around them. If they can achieve what they want in their life then why not You??

Let's start affirming Success and growth along with good health. We all know health is actual wealth...

Chapter 13

Affirmations that can transform your life

- I am worthy of a happy and fulfilling life.
- I am grateful for the abundance of positivity in my life.
- I am deserving of financial prosperity and abundance.
- I am worthy of a healthy, fulfilling, and meaningful relationship.
- I am successful in my career and make a positive impact on those around me.
- I am grateful for my health and take care of my body.
- I am open to new experiences and adventures.
- I am deserving of financial abundance and prosperity.
- I am constantly improving and growing as a person.
- I am worthy of a healthy, fulfilling, and meaningful relationship.
- I am surrounded by positivity and abundance.
- I am surrounded by a supportive and loving community.
- I am confident in my abilities and make decisions with conviction.

- I am grateful for the present moment and live in the present.
- I can manifest my desires and dreams into reality.
- I am worthy of respect and treat myself and others with respect.
- I am grateful for my talents and skills and use them to better myself and the world.
- I am in control of my happiness and create my joy.
- I am grateful for the abundance of Love in life
- I am successful in all areas of my life and constantly strive for excellence.
- I am grateful for my strengths and work on improving my weaknesses.
- I am deserving of a life filled with abundance and prosperity.
- I am confident in my skin and embrace my uniqueness.
- I am surrounded by positive energy and attract positivity into my life.
- I am grateful for my growth and progress and celebrate my victories.
- I am deserving of a fulfilling and meaningful career.
- I am grateful for the abundance of blessings in my life.
- I am capable of creating the life of my dreams.

- I am worthy of forgiveness and extend forgiveness to others.
- I am grateful for my talents and use them to make a positive impact on the world.
- I am confident in my ability to overcome obstacles and achieve success.
- I am worthy of love and respect and cultivate positive relationships.
- I am grateful for the abundance of abundance in my life.
- I am deserving of a healthy and fulfilling lifestyle.
- I am confident in my abilities and trust in my judgment.
- I am grateful for the present moment and live in the present.
- I can create positive change in my life and the world.
- I am worthy of a happy and fulfilling life.
- I am grateful for the abundance of positivity in my life.
- I am deserving of financial prosperity and abundance.
- I am confident in my ability to achieve my goals and dreams.
- I am grateful for the abundance of blessings in my life.
- I am worthy of love and respect and cultivate positive relationships.

- I am deserving of a healthy and fulfilling lifestyle.
- I am confident in my abilities and trust in my judgment.
- I am grateful for the present moment and live in the present.
- I am capable of creating positive change in my life and the world.
- I am worthy of a happy and fulfilling life.
- I am grateful for the abundance of positivity in my life.
- I am deserving of financial prosperity and abundance.
- I am worthy of a healthy, fulfilling, and meaningful relationship.
- I am surrounded by positivity and abundance.
- I am successful in my career and make a positive impact on those around me.
- I am confident in my abilities and make decisions with conviction.
- I am grateful for the present moment and live in the present.
- I can manifest my desires and dreams into reality.
- I am grateful for my health and take care of my body.
- I am open to new experiences and adventures.
- I am deserving of financial abundance and prosperity.

- I am surrounded by a supportive and loving community.
- I am worthy and deserving of love, happiness, and success.
- I am confident and capable of achieving my goals.
- I am strong and capable of overcoming any challenge that comes my way.
- I am grateful for the abundance of opportunities that come my way.
- I am constantly improving and growing as a person.

Chapter 14

Conclusion

Thank you so much readers for sparing your precious time in reading this book. I hope you have gained new insights from the book. We have explored the incredible power of positive affirmations and their transformative effects on our lives. Through understanding the concept of affirmations, exploring their benefits, and providing practical examples, we have delved into the depths of this powerful tool for self-improvement.

Affirmations are not just empty words or wishful thinking. They have the potential to shape our thoughts, beliefs, and actions, guiding us towards a more fulfilling and joyful life. By consciously practising positive affirmations, we can overcome negative self-talk, boost our self-confidence, and cultivate a mindset that attracts success, happiness, and abundance.

Throughout this journey, by incorporating affirmations into our daily routine, we can experience increased self-esteem, improved focus and motivation, reduced stress and anxiety, enhanced overall well-being, and heightened resilience to face life's challenges.

The examples of positive affirmations we have explored are just a glimpse of the infinite possibilities that exist. Whether it is affirming our capabilities, self-worth, happiness, or gratitude, these simple statements have the power to transform our lives from the inside out.

It is important to remember that using affirmations is not a one-time fix. Consistency and commitment are key to harnessing their true power. By integrating them into our daily lives, we can rewire our subconscious minds, replace limiting beliefs with empowering ones, and create a positive and supportive internal dialogue. As we finish this book, I urge you to carry on with your exploration of affirmations. Apply the knowledge and insights you've acquired in your everyday life. Keep in mind that affirmations go beyond being mere words on a page; they serve as instruments for personal development and change.

While engaging in affirmations, you might face instances of uncertainty or resistance. This is a typical and integral aspect of the journey. Embrace these moments as chances for growth, utilizing affirmations to overcome any challenges that may arise. Have confidence in the process and trust in the potency of your affirmations.

Lastly, I want to express my sincere gratitude to you for being on this journey with me. Your commitment to self-improvement and your willingness to explore the power of positive affirmations is truly admirable. I hope that this book has provided you with valuable insights that you can carry with you on your path to personal growth and happiness. Remember, the power to create the life you desire lies within you. Harness the power of positive affirmations, embrace your true potential, and live a life filled with joy, abundance, and fulfillment.

Inject more positive energy and turn your life around by practicing these 7 small habits each day:

1. **Adopt a growth mindset:** Henry Ford once said: *"Whether you think you can, or you think you can't - you're right."* What does this mean? It means that the view you have of yourself will profoundly affect the way you lead your life. For example, if you believe you can think more positively, you can make it happen. Conversely, if you don't believe in the power of positive thinking, then it doesn't matter how much others will tell you how great the benefits are. How can you think more positively? Start nurturing a "growth mindset" (versus a fixed mindset). If there's something about your mindset you don't like, the good news is - you can change it for the better.

2. **Say "thank you" to change your attitude about life:** Practicing gratitude rewires our brain to think about positive things, the things that we have going for us, instead of the things we do not have and that can leave us feeling frustrated and unhappy. How? Create a gratitude journal and write in it for 5 minutes each morning when you wake up or just before you go to sleep. **List 3 things you are grateful for in your life right now.** It can be the simplest of things, such as having a warm bed to sleep in, a roof over your head, a family that loves you, food in your fridge, a dog or cat that you have as your pet. Get specific: if it's a family member or a close friend, write down which of their qualities you are grateful for.

3. **Treat happiness like a habit you can consistently work on:** A happy life cannot exist without you creating it. What does that mean? It means that every day you need to actively look for what you can do to become happier, instead of expecting life to just become happy on its own. How can you do this? Apply some positive psychology to the way you lead your life, and you will feel a more positive impact on your attitude, your motivation, and your relationships with people.

4. **Instead of saying "I can't do this right now!" say "Why not?":** We may feel that we can't do something out of fear, intimidation, reluctance to change the status quo, even just because it feels natural to resist to act. It's all part of being human. Try working through it with these steps:

- **Think carefully if there is something else hiding behind procrastination.** Maybe it is simply the fear of not being able to do something successfully.

- Next time you feel like saying "I can't," **ask yourself where the resistance is coming from**. Be honest with yourself. Find out what it is so you can do something about it.

- **Think about the benefit of changing your reaction: whenever you say "why not?" you win over fear.** There is something powerful when we leave a little space open for possibilities, instead of shutting the door in our own face. It's a subtle change in attitude towards ourselves than can have a tremendous impact in our lives.

5. **See your mistakes in a more positive light:** Making mistakes is a normal part of life. It is how you approach them that matters. Try a different strategy of viewing your past by forgiving yourself for mistakes that you made. Reflect on them, learn from them, but don't hold on to them. This applies to your relationships, your career, your education, and other areas of your life in which you feel you didn't achieve what you wanted or underperformed in some way. By changing how you relate to mistakes, you will give yourself more freedom to manage your future more successfully.

6. **Eliminate toxic people from your life:** Toxic people may claim they are your friends, but they are not. What makes them toxic is their negative attitude towards everything, so it's not likely they can give you a boost of positivity. **Be very selective who you spend your free time with, and next time a toxic person wants to monopolize your time, just say no.** Tell them you're busy. Don't engage in negative banter. You're better off spending free time on your own doing something that makes you relaxed and happy.

7. **Get in touch with the best version of yourself:** Instead of being overly self-critical about everything you do (or everything you feel

you've done wrong), look more closely at the best version of yourself. You know who that is. It's that version of you that you strive to be, that you've always wanted to be. It's the version of you who knows what is right, what needs to be done, how much time needs to be sacrificed, which goals need to be pursued. Always keep a conversation going between the self you currently are and your ideal self. Whenever you are contemplating your next move, ask the best version of yourself what is the right path to take, then go in that direction. When you see yourself in a more positive light, you increase your motivation to accomplish the goals you set for yourself - the ones that are truly the most important to you.

Final tip:

Read Viktor E. Frankl's book "Man's Search for Meaning" It's a book that goes beyond positive thinking and provides an in-depth look at the psychology of survival. It is a real-life story by a psychiatrist and Holocaust survivor about finding strength to live in circumstances where most people would give up. It is also one of the most humbling reading experiences and a must read.

Wishing you a journey filled with love, growth, and endless possibilities.

A Humble Appeal

I shall be grateful if you would share your valuable feedback on any aspect of this book. If you have any suggestions in your mind, you are always welcome. It will be a great help to me. Please feel free to discuss.

You can submit your feedback at

virdi.ravinder@yahoo.in

About the Author

Born and brought up in Ludhiana, Ravinder Kaur comes from a middle-class family and has wonderful Life experiences. She resides in Kharar, Punjab, with her lovely family. Ravinder Kaur is the author of several books, including Live Life as Your Last Inning, Positive Alphabets of Life, Quit Like a Strong Woman, The Power of Wisdom, The Power of New ABC and 28 Days of Inspiration. She enjoys being in nature since she is a keen observer. Ravinder Kaur is enthusiastic about writing to make a difference in the world, and she aspires to continue inspiring and empowering people to act for a better future.

May I ask you for a small favour?

I want to give you a big thanks for taking out time to read this book. You could have chosen any other book, but you took mine, and I appreciate this. I hope you got at least a few actionable insights that will have a positive impact on your day-to-day life.

Can I ask for 30 seconds more of your time?

I would love it if you could leave a <u>review</u> about the book. Reviews may not matter to big-name authors; but they are a tremendous help for authors like me, who don't have much following. They help me to grow my readership by encouraging folks to take a chance on my books.

To put it straight – <u>Reviews are the lifeblood for any author.</u>

It will just take less than a minute of your time, but will tremendously help me to reach out to more people, so please leave your review. Thanks for your support. And I would love to see your review.

My Other Books

Live Life as Your Last Inning

Life is a beautiful journey of taking small steps at the right time to live happily and to the fullest. If you wish to ignite your mind; set the purpose, and fuel your dreams the ride of life is just for you. Give it wings to fly higher and higher. This book is intended to inspire you for a higher level, which you have put off for another day. Get ready to mentor yourself with simple tips and ways that will help you to change your outlook. And make your life worth living and give a new meaning to your life. Live your life as your last innings as every day is your last day; live life as no one lived and leave a legacy behind you....

Positive Alphabets of Life

If you wish to ignite the spark in your mind, then be ready for the surprise. Positive alphabets of life is a unique effort to change your perspective and give you a new outlook to transform the world. Life will change automatically once you follow these alphabets and adopt them in routine life then you will see a definite change in your thinking. Get ready to mentor yourself with these positive alphabets. This book explains a new and unique meaning to our traditional ABC simply and interestingly. A comprehensive book that inspires and motivates you and answers the following question:

- Do you think your Positive Attitude will lead you to focus on your goals?
- Whether your Optimism will keep you determined and persistent?
- How Zeal of a person can decide the future course of action?
- How Xenial behaviour will motivate you to help others?
- Do you think feeling grateful to God can impact you all?

Quit Like a Strong Woman

Does the perfect relation start with friendship or love? *Not every story has a happy or sad ending.*

How it will be if this story ends with a unique relation? *What will be the uniqueness of that relation?*

Will Shalini get a good friend or a life partner in her lifetime? A sweet dramatic story revolves around Shalini and her life's decisions.

Life was never smooth for her. She is a strong woman but still needs someone in her life. She has gone through various ups and downs in life but stood still even in tough time.

What will happen when she meets Mehak? A unique twist will create a unique end to this story.

The Power of Wisdom

"The Power of Wisdom" shows that our emotional, psychological, mental and spiritual health is influenced by how comfortable we are navigating unknown areas of our lives. It takes a fresh look at the importance of wisdom in personal development, relationships, leadership, and success. This book serves as a mentor to help you walk in wisdom on your journey to a healthy, meaningful, and transformed life. This book will assist you in navigating life's problems, making better decisions, and cultivating inner peace and pleasure.

Whether you are a student, a professional, or a leader, this book will encourage you to tap into your inner wisdom, unleash your true power and enjoy relevant insights for your daily life.

Live Life as Your Last Inning - Workbook

Discover **"Workbook - Live Life as Your Last Inning,"** the practical implementation of the main book **"Live Life as Your Last Inning."**

Explore meaningful exercises, set achievable goals, and embrace a mindset of gratitude.

Whether you're in the first inning or the ninth, this workbook will help you make the most of every moment, ensuring your life is a grand slam of happiness and fulfillment.

Unlock the secrets to a more fulfilling life with the **"Live Life as Your Last Inning - Workbook."**

Shalini

क्या सही रिश्ता दोस्ती या प्यार से शुरू होता है?

हर कहानी का सुखद या दुखद अंत नहीं होता।

कैसा रहेगा अगर इस कहानी का अंत एक अनोखे रिश्ते से हो?

उस रिश्ते की विशिष्टता क्या होगी? क्या शालिनी को अपने जीवनकाल में एक अच्छा दोस्त या जीवन साथी मिलेगा?

शालिनी और उसके जीवन के फैसलों के इर्द-गिर्द एक प्यारी नाटकीय कहानी घूमती है। उसके लिए जीवन कभी सहज नहीं था। वह एक मजबूत महिला हैं लेकिन फिर भी उसे अपने जीवन में किसी की जरूरत है। वह जीवन में कई उतार-चढ़ाव से गुजरी हैं लेकिन कठिन समय में भी डटी रहीं।

क्या होगा जब वह महक से मिलेंगी?

एक अनोखा मोड़ इस कहानी का एक अनूठा अंत बनाएगा।

The Power of New ABC

In a world driven by fast-paced technology and the desire for shortcuts, "The Power of New ABC" provides a unique perspective that promises to excite your imagination. This fascinating book takes you on a trip from ancient times to present times, illustrating the significant changes in English alphabet and their impact on people's lives. You will find a unique collection of alphabets within its pages that can alter your thoughts and reshape your environment. This book redefines the conventional ABCs and explains how these new alphabets may lead to success and fulfillment in your life, from Positive Attitude to Zeal. By incorporating these alphabets into your everyday routine, you will notice a significant difference in your thinking and approach to life. New Alphabets with New and Positive Meaning.

28 Days of Inspiration

Embark on a transformative journey with "28 Days of Inspiration," a unique guide designed to ignite your creativity, cultivate mindfulness, and awaken your inner potential. In a world filled with hustle and bustle, this book serves as a beacon of inspiration, offering a month-long expedition into the realms of self-discovery and personal growth. "28 Days of Inspiration" is not merely a book; it is a companion on your quest for a more inspired and purposeful life. The book doesn't just stop at inspiration; it delves into the practical aspects of turning ideas into action. It is a call to action, an invitation to embark on a transformative journey that promises not just inspiration, but a renewed sense of purpose and a richer, more vibrant life. Open these pages and let the journey begin.

References

https://www.psychologytoday.com/
https://netofferbd.com/
https://www.wikipedia.org/